SILVER LATIN EPIC

SILVER LATIN EPIC

A Selection from Lucan,
Valerius Flaccus,
Silius Italicus
& Statius

Edited by

H. MacL. Currie

Bristol Classical Press

This impression 2004
First published in 1985 by
Bristol Classical Press
an imprint of
Gerald Duckworth & Co. Ltd.
90-93 Cowcross Street, London EC1M 6BF
Tel: 020 7490 7300
Fax: 020 7490 0080
inquiries@duckworth-publishers.co.uk
www.ducknet.co.uk

ISBN 0 906515 37 8

Cover illustration: Athena watching Jason
being disgorged by the dragon; painting by Douris
on a late Archaic red-figure cup, Vatican Museums.
(Drawing by Elizabeth Induni.)

Printed and bound in Great Britain by
Antony Rowe Ltd, Eastbourne

CONTENTS

LIST OF PASSAGES

FOREWORD

This volume aims to offer for use of sixth-formers and
undergraduates a representative annotated range of passages
from the Silver Latin epic poets - Lucan, Valerius Flaccus,
Silius Italicus and Statius. This is a body of poetry that
tends to be familiar only to specialists, which is a pity,
for it has its merits.

The literature of the period between the death of Augustus
(A.D. 14) and the ascent to the throne of Hadrian (A.D. 117),
the 'Silver Age', is overshadowed by a great past already
recognised as classical. The proscription of Silver Latin
took place during the nineteenth century when the canon of
Greek and Latin authors underwent critical assessment; the
indiscriminate reading of the seventeenth and eighteenth
centuries was at an end. But the application of the adjective
'Silver' - as opposed to 'Golden' for the high literary
achievements of the first century B.C. - has a disparaging
effect which is not at all deserved, as readers of Tacitus
and Juvenal will testify.

Change, however, and eventually a decline did set in. In
epic Virgil was pre-eminent and had attained 'classical'
status even within his own life-time. He had a vast influence
upon the subsequent development of both poetry and prose; the
two media drew closer together as writers of each looked to
him as a common model and inspiration. The four Silver epic
poets represented in this volume were deeply conscious of
the *Aeneid*. Lucan reacted to it - or against it - by follow-
ing the annalistic tradition, choosing the civil war between
Caesar and Pompey as his subject, abandoning divine inter-
vention - or, rather, replacing it with an emphasis on the
occult and the bizarre - and deploying a strikingly abundant
rhetorical style. Valerius and Statius chose Greek mytholog-
ical themes on which they strongly imprinted their own poetic

personalities. Silius took as his subject the historical
struggle against Hannibal but adopted the Homeric and
Virgilian scheme in which dissensions amongst men are par-
alleled by animosities amongst the gods who each have their
human favourites; his admiration for Virgil was idolatrous
and his *Punica* is filled with not always well-judged imi-
tations.

However independent the four poets may have wished or tried
to be, the existence of Virgil could not be ignored; his
challenge had somehow to be met. Most of the passages in
this volume recall or invite comparison with some Virgilian
episode. That these episodes are from the most commonly
read books of the *Aeneid* is intended to provide added inter-
est and an appendix of Virgilian passages for comparative
study has been included. The superiority of Virgil is often
easy to discern but, though he surpasses in scope and art
his Silver Age successors, their "humbler creation" should
not be thought negligible.

Each of the Silver epic poets has individual qualities. To
look upon them as mere foils to Virgil is a mistake. Some-
times, in the course of sustained passages, Lucan achieves
an elevation of tone and utterance which can be moving, though
rhetorical pressures may limit its duration. This is perhaps
illustrated by passages 3 and 5 below or by 1.67-182 on the
causes of the civil war, 2.67-113 on the precedent of
Marius, 7.385-459 on the fatal consequences of the battle
of Pharsalia, 8.560-636 on the murder of Pompey, 8.708-
822 on the burial of Pompey's headless corpse (cf. pas-
sage 6 below), and 10.53-171 on the banquet of Caesar and
Cleopatra. The longest excerpt given in this volume, the
episode of Amyclas (passage 5 below), is typical of the poet
in its blend of description, moralising and rhetoric.

Valerius Flaccus is probably the most poetical of the four
poets. His freshness and originality appear not least in his

handling of Jason. Hull (1979) states (407): "Jason's personality is a unifying factor throughout the poem as we have it, and goes a long way in counteracting the effects of what H. J. Rose called the descent of the latter part of the saga from 'the clear atmosphere of Homeric exploits to mean and treacherous magic and intrigue'(A Handbook of Greek Mythology 203)." The development of the love affair between Jason and Medea is also sensitively handled by Valerius (passages 11-16 below).

Silius Italicus is normally heavy-handed but, on occasion, capable of a certain refinement of perception (passages 17 and 22 below).

Silver poets generally needed space to have their say. In his Thebaid, that allegorical epic with a Stoic framework - see Vessey (1973) - Statius wished to create a vivid impression of the foulness which arises from the conflict of human passions before the final book in which virtue triumphs. He is not afraid to spread himself to achieve this aim. He is a clear observer and is at his best in small scenes and detailed presentations. This is in strong contrast to Lucan, who moves, as Nisard observed, from word to thing - i.e. the mode of expression takes precedence over accuracy of description. Passages 25, 29 and 30 below particularly illustrate Statius' capacity to convey effectively feeling or atmosphere in a few words.

The scanty fragment of Statius' Achilleid is much simpler in style than his Thebaid and is suffused, as in the portrait of the young Achilles disguised as a girl of Scyros (passage 32 below), with a romantic tenderness reminiscent of Hellenistic art and literature when it treats the humanisation of a divinity.

Poetry there is in the Silver Latin epics but it comes not

in strong and steady rays, rather in fitful gleams.

The text used in this volume is eclectic. The biblio-
graphy is selective; a complete one would have been long
indeed. To the work of previous commentators I am happy
to acknowledge my great indebtedness. Much editorial assis-
tance has been rendered by John Betts; layout is by Amanda
Barrett and Jane Bircher and the cover illustration is
by Jean Bees. My best thanks, also, to Gordon Birch for
his help with the proofs.

H. MacL. C.
July, 1984.

INTRODUCTION

I   THE ASCENDANCY OF RHETORIC

§1   "A man", said Oscar Wilde, "would need a heart of stone not
to laugh at the death of Little Nell". He was referring to
the lack of restraint which Dickens shows in his treatment
of this episode in *The Old Curiosity Shop*. Pathos is ap-
plied unsparingly.

§2   Such excess is not the mark of "classicism" at its most
highly developed. The great classical writers of Greece
and Rome - those who were and are acknowledged as belonging
to the front rank, who laid down a standard - are dis-
tinguished by reserve, by a disinclination to try to say
everything, by a preference for the general over the
particular. The Ciceronian and Augustan eras represent
a kind of "classicism" - a "Golden Age" of achievement
in Latin literature. The succeeding "Silver Age", from
the death of Augustus in A.D. 14 to the accession of
Hadrian in A.D. 117, sees a change of manner in liter-
ature. All the big things seemed to have been done.
Writers looked for a way of challenging their great
predecessors; they found it in form and technique. The
emphasis now tended to be more on the mode of expression
than on the subject-matter itself - on the "how" rather
than the "what". The sway of rhetoric, which was already
established as the substance of secondary education, had
become predominant. Under the principate the curtail-
ment of real opportunities in the *forum* had caused
orators to seek an outlet for their talents in artificial
excercises, in which the need to be arresting through
bold forms of expression and ingenuity of argument was
held to be paramount.[1] Rhetorical mannerism permeates
Silver Latin literature; emphasis upon the mode of
expression, exaggeration, lack of proportion and taste
are common features. But this is not the whole story.

§3   Modern criticism of Silver Latin literature has not done
it justice. Its faults are seen easily enough but it
should be recalled that the age produced Tacitus and
Juvenal, two of the most impressive figures of Latin
literature. The zealous search for striking locutions
and challenging epigrams may at times seem tiresome,
especially to the modern ear whose expectations may be
more austere. A style which has the capacity to deal
"verbal *coups de théâtre*" can excite the imagination,
even if at times it may go on too long and "tear a
passion to tatters". We should not quarrel about tastes,

---

[1] See §29-42 below; and for declamatory practice and its influence on
poetry, with significant examples from Ovid, Lucan and Juvenal, see
Winterbottom (1979).

but we ought at least to reflect on the conditions and attitudes which created this style. Declamation bred a taste for descriptive digressions which became a necessary part of the declaimer's and of the poet's stock-in-trade; the artistry with which they were managed was of great interest to the cultivated public. Descriptive digression or *ekphrasis* had a long history going back to Homer and the digressions of Lucan or Statius, however insipid or irrelevant they may now appear, should be read as intended embellishments, having a precise literary function within the economy of the whole to enhance the work and impart to it the character of a flourishing tree with many branches.[2]

§4 One generation is separated from its predecessor by changes in sensibility. The poetry of Eliot and Pound with its obscurities and ambiguities, its harshness and atonal qualities, was a reaction against the smooth harmonies and ceremoniousness of much Victorian versification. New ways of exploring experience and truth were being discovered. The epic poets of the Silver Age knew Virgil thoroughly but their path lay in a different direction. Stylistic elaboration is not in favour today, rather the simple, the direct, the conversational; it is illuminating to compare the daily paragraphs of *The Times* of a century ago with those of the same newspaper today. The rhetorically based writings of the Silver Age should be approached with a sympathetic understanding of the conventions and standards that governed their production. Verbal dexterity, the well-turned epigram, were positive accomplishments, however obtrusive, even repulsive, they may seem today. Mediaeval and Renaissance literature drew much inspiration from Silver Age poetry (and prose), and if Dante and Chaucer found Lucan and Statius admirable as models, we should at least give them patient understanding, even when we cannot share the admiration.

§5 It is unwise, too, to treat Silver Latin as an isolated phenomenon; for if we do so there is a danger of highlighting its flaws to an unnecessary extent. Many of its characteristics are continuations or extensions of features present in Golden Age literature. The somewhat contrived quality of Horace in places is taken up by Persius and Statius; Ovid's ingenious flexibility of expression points forward to Seneca and Lucan; features of the prose style of Sallust and Livy anticipate Tacitus. Silver latinity (see §28 below) is part of a broader developing organism. In the

---

[2] A. M. F. Gunn, *The Mirror of Love* (Texas, 1952), traces the same phenomenon in mediaeval literature and sees it as an expression of impulses found in the embellishment of contemporary architecture and decorative art.

last analysis literature is an artificial product. We
have to make allowances in our assessment of it. Trad-
ition, aesthetic intention, the pressures of contemporary
fashion are amongst the major factors which influence an
author and they should all be recalled in any assessment
of his literary output. If there is *ekphrasis*, if there
is self-conscious artistry and contrivance in language
and structure, if there is a great deal of rhetoric in
Silver epic, it is to be expected and to be appreciated
on its own terms.

II THE SILVER EPIC POETS

Latin Epic before the Silver Age

§6 Prior to Virgil's *Aeneid* the verse chronicle - a Greek
invention - seems to have been the usual form for Latin
epic. Only scanty fragments remain. The *Bellum Punicum*,
a verse history of the First Punic war by CN. NAEVIUS
(ca. 269-199 B.C.), was written in the ancient Latin
metre (based on accent) called "Saturnian". But the
history of Latin epic really begins with the *Annales*
of Q. ENNIUS (239-169 B.C.), a Calabrian who obtained
Roman citizenship in 184 B.C. Ennius used, for the first
time in Italy, the hexameter verse of Homer, adapting it
by bold experiment to the less tripping, more stately
rhythms of the Latin language. From Homer, too, he drew
the machinery by which the gods involve themselves in
human affairs. Only some six hundred lines of the
Annales survive,[3] though the poem was originally a vast
composition in eighteen books, whose essence is conveyed
in the celebrated line: *moribus antiquis stat res Romana
virisque*. Ennius undertook to write the history of Rome
from its foundation to his own day - a national poem
which was above all to be a glorification of Roman
character. His title was drawn from the old city
chronicles, the *annales* of the priests, a year by year
record which was also used by the pioneering Roman
historians (who wrote in Greek), Q. Fabius Pictor and
L. Cincius Alimentus, at the time of the Second Punic
War.

§7 The annalistic epic tended, of necessity, to be a chrono-
logical catalogue; even the inclusion of divine inter-
vention could not alter that. VIRGIL (P. Vergilius
Maro 70-19 B.C.) struck out on an entirely fresh path in
the *Aeneid*, which set the achievements of Augustus with-
in a mythological and historical context. In it the
members of the *gens Julia* saw themselves as descended

---

[3] Most conveniently collected, along with the fragments of Naevius,
in Warmington (1957).

from the Trojan hero Aeneas and his son Ascanius
or Iulus; in Aeneas' mother Venus they worshipped
the divine ancestress of the family. Augustus
could, therefore, be connected with the Aeneas legend;
and, though generations of annalists had already treated
the tale which associated Aeneas with the beginnings of
Rome, the direct link with Augustus provided a new
emphasis. Virgil's epic was a national poem which also
comprehensively expressed the spiritual and cultural
heritage of the Greco-Roman world, offering a rich and
subtle blend of history, legend, religion and philo-
sophy.

M. Annaeus Lucanus

§8 Lucan (A.D. 39-65), grandson of the elder Seneca and
nephew of the younger, was trained by the Stoic
philosopher Cornutus and later studied in Athens.
Stoicism was the prevailing ideology at Rome during the
first and second centuries A.D. and Lucan was
noticeably influenced by his Stoic uncle, the younger
Seneca. In his epic, republican idealism is set within
a Stoic framework. His interpretation of Fate (*fatum,*
as in Virgil) as a force which tests men by drawing
out their strengths and weaknesses is closely
paralleled in the writings of his uncle, especially the
de Providentia.

§9 Augustus had encouraged and lived on terms of intimacy
with poets and men of letters. Such patronage was
hardly a mark of the reigns of his successors Tiberius,
Caligula (Gaius) and Claudius. Nero, however, convinced
of literary genius within himself, reverted to the practice
of Augustus. Lucan gained Nero's favourable attention
through his literary and rhetorical ability but, before
long, feeling jealous of Lucan's gifts, the emperor for-
bade him to give further public recitations of his poetry.
This, along with his growing hatred of Nero's despotic
principate, led Lucan in A.D. 65 to join the conspiracy
of C. Calpurnius Piso organised to assassinate the
emperor. The conspiracy was discovered and Lucan was
forced to commit suicide. As the first three books of the
de Bello Civili were published separately,[4] the fulsome
invocation to Nero at the start of Book 1 (passage 1
below) was not intended as ironic or satirical but
genuinely reflects the optimism with which Lucan (and
others) greeted the early years of Nero's principate.
The literary renaissance was a hopeful omen for the future.
But for Lucan disillusionment set in and after Book 3 the
tone changes to one of moral condemnation. In the figure

---

[4] Dilke (1960) 5, n. 3.

of Julius Caesar he sums up all the evils of the
imperial system and his deepening sense of regret for
the former republic.

§10 The title of Lucan's epic in the manuscripts is *de
Bello Civili* but it is better known as the *Pharsalia*
because of its vivid account of the battle of Pharsalus
in Book 7. It treats the civil war between Caesar and
Pompey in ten books - the last unfinished, ending
abruptly at 10.546. Book 1 and part of 2 are intro-
ductory; then he describes Pompey's flight from Italy.
Book 3 deals with Caesar's activities at Rome and the
siege of Massilia (Marseilles); 4 with the fighting
round Ilerda. Manoeuvres in Epirus take up Books 5
and 6 and lead in 7 to the battle of Pharsalus; 8-10
treat Pompey's flight and death, Cato's last stand in
Africa and Caesar's presence at Alexandria.

§11 In his overtly historical subject matter Lucan looks
back beyond Virgil to Ennius and the annalistic
tradition. Unlike Ennius, however, he rejects divine
machinery, replacing it to some extent with magic and
the occult, oracles, prodigies and omens; no book of the
poem is without evidence of Lucan's interest in these
matters.[5] At the same time the operation of *fatum* on
the affairs of men constantly receives strong emphasis;
at the outset of the poem, for instance, in discussing
the inevitability of civil war, Lucan pessimistically
concludes (1.70) that nothing great is allowed to survive
- *summisque negatum stare diu* - because of the envy of
Fate. Each of the central figures, Cato, Caesar and
Pompey, is shown reacting to the strokes of Fate. Cato,
the soldierly sage, resolutely continues (Book 9) the
hopeless struggle after Pompey's death. Pompey himself
grows in moral stature from the first book, where the
poet wonders (1.126-127) which of the protagonists more
justly took up arms, until the eighth, where he resignedly
boards the Egyptian boat with the strong suspicion that
his own assassination will be the outcome (8.560-636).
Julius Caesar is presented as egotistical, possessed by
a deep sense of his own personal *Fortuna*; his great (and
historically attested) constructive dynamism Lucan
ignores or cannot see.

§12 It is often said that the *de Bello Civili* lacks unity,
that it has no central epic hero. The emphasis shifts
from Pompey to Caesar, back to Pompey and then to Cato
and the poem proceeds episodically: a series of major
conflicts - Caesar's march on Rome, the siege of Massilia,

---

[5] e.g. Book 5 - the long digression on Appius' consultation of the
Delphic oracle; or Book 6 - the horrific episode in which Sextus
Pompeius consults the Thessalian witch Erichtho.

the Ilerda campaign, the defeat of Curio in Africa,
Pompey's escape from Caesar's grasp in Epirus - cul-
minates in the battle of Pharsalus which Lucan sees as
peculiarly critical for Roman history. Historical nar-
ration following events in order would give the poem
unity of one sort; the selectivity which Lucan practises
gives it another unity - one which is artistic and emot-
ional. Pharsalus and all that it means for Rome becomes
the focal point of the whole epic, a disastrous blow in-
flicted by fate. In one sense the victim and the "hero"
of the poem is Rome herself.

§13 The influence of Virgil on Lucan's epic was considerable.
For instance, Sextus Pompeius' consultation of the Thes-
salian witch Erichtho (Book 6) is a highly coloured counter-
part to Aeneas' descent to consult his father in Hades in
Aeneid 6. The invocation to Nero (1.33-66 - passage 1
below) is clearly motivated by a passage from the *Georgics*
in honour of Augustus (1.24-42 - Appendix passage a below).

§14 The *de Bello Civili* is the unfinished work of a young man
and must be judged in that light. Lucan is not on the
basis of it a poet of the first order, but he had a wide
command of rhetoric and great intellectual energy, along
with remarkable political and historical insight. On
occasion his rhetoric can rise to fine poetry but equally
his use of irrelevant erudition (see §§42-43 below) in
the form of descriptive digressions can be tedious.
Lucan lacks Virgil's profound understanding of human suf-
fering but he does nonetheless manage to sustain a clear
human interest throughout his narrative.

§15 In the Middle Ages Lucan was a popular author. Later,
Christopher Marlowe published a translation of the first
book (1600). Corneille and other French dramatists of
the seventeenth century were impressed by *de Bello Civili*.
Samuel Johnson hailed Nicholas Rowe's translation (1718)
as "one of the greatest productions of English poetry".
Southey and Shelley in their earlier years both even pre-
ferred - or affected to prefer - Lucan to Virgil.

C. *Valerius Flaccus*

§16 Of the life of Valerius Flaccus we know virtually nothing.
Quintilian (10.1.90) considers his death, which must have
occurred about A.D. 96, a severe loss to literature. It is
clear that Vespasian (A.D. 69-79) was living at the time
when Valerius began his epic; the poem's prologue clearly
refers to him, but it also refers to his sons Titus (A.D.
79-81) and Domitian (A.D. 81-96). Vespasian, Titus and
Domitian together comprise the Flavian dynasty, under
which there took place something of a literary revival.

§17 Valerius' *Argonautica* describes Jason's quest for the
Golden Fleece, his success with the help of Medea, and
their subsequent escape together from Chalcis. The poem
breaks off abruptly in the middle of the eighth book.
Like Lucan and Silius Italicus, Valerius published some
early books not long after they were written;[6] whether
the poem was incomplete at Valerius' death or has simply
survived incomplete we cannot say.

§18 As Lucan had eluded the ascendancy held by Virgil's
Aeneid by choice of subject and method, so Valerius
tried to evade it by treating a specifically Greek legend
in his epic. The poem is based on the *Argonautica* of
the Alexandrian poet Apollonius of Rhodes, but Valerius
allows himself great freedom in handling his source.
Apollonius was a learned poet in the Alexandrian tradition
and enjoyed displaying his erudition; Valerius' interests
lie elsewhere. He is highly poetical, showing a strong
faculty for picturesque description and a controlled imagi-
nation which keeps his heroes human beings. His pre-
sentation of the love story of Medea and Jason shows fine
psychological perception.

§19 Valerius has at times an allusiveness in description which
is very effective. For instance, his handling (6.182-188)
of a traditional set piece, the beginning of a battle,
contains features which had descended from Homer, Virgil,
Lucan and elsewhere, but it remains brief and striking:

> *illi ubi consertis iunxere frementia telis*
> *agmina virque virum galeis adflavit adactis,*
> *continuo hinc obitus perfractaque caedibus arma*
> *corporaque, alternus cruor alternaeque ruinae;*
> *volvit ager galeas et thorax egerit imbres*
> *sanguineos; hinc barbarici glomerantur ovatus,*
> *hinc gemitus, mixtaeque virum cum pulvere vitae.*

Here *consertis ... telis* is drawn from Lucan (7.520), while
virque virum is Virgilian (*Aeneid* 10.361 - *haeret pede pes
densusque viro vir*; 11.631-635 = Appendix passage b below -
a passage which had profound influence upon treatments of
the topic). On the other hand *adflavit* - 'man breathed on
man when helmets had been forced together' - is Valerius'
own touch of originality; so too is the pathos of *vitae* for
cadavera in the final line quoted above. Bold novelty of
expression is not infrequent: *totusque dei* - 'possessed by
the god' - (1.207); *iniqui/nube meri* - (of a mind) 'clouded
with excess of wine' - (3.65f.); *et magnae pelago tremit
umbra Sinopes* - 'and the shadow of huge Sinope trembles

---

[6] Strand (1972) 7-38.

over the sea' - (5.108); *et tandem virgine cessit* - 'and
at last gave up his claim to the maiden' (referring to
Styrus who has been drowned) - (8.368). Statius later
finds inspiration in Valerius' linguistic compactness
and dexterity. Along with his allusive brevity and neat
originality, there is in Valerius an avoidance of the
horrific on which Lucan and Statius sometimes liked to
dwell. For instance he incorporated (2.82-427) on a
modest scale the story of the Lemnian women but does not
go into gruesome detail about how they murdered their
husbands; this is in strong contrast to Statius who
irrelevantly expands his treatment of the same story in
the *Thebaid* into almost three books (4.646-7.226) - an
account which is very highly coloured, emotional and
horrific.

Ti. Catius Asconius Silius Italicus

§20 Silius Italicus was born in A.D. 25. His *Punica* was
composed in the later years of the Flavian emperor
Domitian (A.D. 81-96). Having served as Nero's last
consul in A.D. 68 and then as a proconsul in Asia, Silius
retired to his fine estates, indulging a deep and romantic
interest in the past. He acquired Cicero's villa at
Tusculum and his estate at Naples included the grave of
Virgil. There he died, probably in A.D. 101, by his own
hand while suffering from an incurable tumour.

§21 The *Punica* deals with the Second Punic War and its cam-
paigns against Hannibal. Essentially it follows Livy's
account. In seventeen books comprising upwards of 12,000
lines, it is our longest surviving Latin poem. Like Lucan
and Valerius Flaccus, Silius clearly published some of his
early books together quite soon after composition. In the
manner of Virgil he shows a worried Venus consulting Jupiter
about the untrustworthy Carthaginians and their threatened
expansion to the detriment of Rome. In his reply Jupiter
covers future Roman history down to Vespasian in nine lines;
thirteen lines on Vespasian and Titus follow; then twenty-
three on Domitian, hailing him as military hero, orator,
poet and destined divinity (3.557-629).

§22 Silius' style is mainly prosaic. On occasion he achieves
a certain dignity, even beauty, but he has little claim
to originality. His *Punica* represents a return to the
historical epic of Lucan but, in contrast to Lucan, Silius
makes much use of the divine machinery of Homer, Ennius
and Virgil. His admiration for Virgil is everywhere
apparent. He even has Scipio, after the deaths of his
father and uncle in Spain, make a descent from Avernus
(where he has been resting) to the underworld (13.400-895)
- his own equivalent to *Aeneid* 6. But the episode includes
Homeric elements and Scipio meets the Greek poet surrounded

by his epic heroes amongst the shades (passage 21 below).

P. Papinius Statius

§23 Statius was born in A.D. 45 at Naples where his father,
to whom he was devoted (*Silvae* 5.3), was a schoolmaster
(and poet). He moved to Rome and, like Valerius, took
part in the literary upsurge under Domitian. The *Silvae*
are occasional poems, mostly commissioned for people
belonging to the emperor's circle, on whom Statius was
to some extent dependent, but also for other distinguished
friends - descriptions of their property (villas, art
treasures, baths), congratulations, and poetic obituaries.
Praise of the emperor had by now become a recognised liter-
ary topic in which poets vied with one another to exploit
ingenious turns of speech and thought; some of Statius'
flattery now seems immoderate (*Silvae* 4.1-3). The em-
peror's German campaigns were the subject of another poem
by Statius (now lost). The poet had an estate at Alba
which acquired its running water through Domitian's good
graces (*Silvae* 3.1.61ff.) and where his father was buried
(5.3.35-40). Towards the end of his life Statius retired
to his native city where he died in A.D. 96, apparently
before the death of the emperor in the same year.

§24 The *Silvae,* published from A.D. 92 onwards, have a certain
charm and dexterity but their chief value is as documents
illustrating the social history of the Flavian age. Most
of our information, too, about the poet's life is drawn
from them but generally from passing remarks; for the poet
rarely speaks personally. A notable exception is the
moving poem to *Somnus* (5.4 - see Appendix passage s
below). 2.7 is a posthumous birthday ode in honour
of Lucan, addressed to his widow Polla, and highly appre-
ciative of that poet's worth.

§25 In the field of epic Statius imitated not only Virgil,
whom he regarded as pre-eminent,[7] but also Lucan, the
most independent of the Silver epic poets, and to some
extent Ovid (see §30 below). But he ignored the Alex-
andrian poets, looking back rather to Sophocles and cyclic
epic (a collective name for certain Greek poems, neither
Homeric nor Hesiodic, but dating between the ninth and
sixth centuries B.C.). The *Thebaid*, published in A.D. 91,
is in twelve books and deals with the theme of "seven
against Thebes", the fratricidal quarrel between Eteocles
and Polynices. The preliminaries occupy ten books and the
actual contests of the brothers and their consequences are
pressed into two. Divine machinery is extensively used

---

[7] *Thebaid* 12.816-7 - *vive, precor, nec tu divinam Aeneida tempta,/
sed longe sequere et vestigia semper adora.*

and the whole poem is constructed as a series of episodes, the longest being the story of Hypsipyle and the Lemnian women which extends from 4.464 to 7.226 and is a small epic in itself. The episode has its own unity through ring composition (by which an initial motif recurs at the end): Bacchus is prominent at the start and at the conclusion he re-appears making pleas to Jupiter. By contrast, Valerius Flaccus' handling of the same theme - organically part of the plot, as it is not in Statius - has a characteristic brevity (see §19 above). Diffuse though the *Thebaid* may be, it is held together by ring composition, which relates the first and last books. There is a balance between the tyranny of Eteocles and that of Polynices; and between the night journey of Polynices in Book 1 from Thebes and the night journey of his wife Argia in Book 12 to the same city. *Ekphrasis* (see §3 above; introductory notes to passage 10 below) is frequent in the *Thebaid*: e.g. description of a sacred grove (4.419-442); the House of Sleep (10.84-115 - see introductory note to passage 31 below); or of the altar of *Clementia* in Athens (12.481-511). Statius shares with Lucan a love of pedantry but can carry it to even more ridiculous lengths: e.g. possible reasons why the earth opened for Amphiaraus (7.809-816); or speculations on the cause of Capaneus' *furor* (10.831-836).

§26 Allegorical personification is much used by Statius. It was already a feature of earlier Latin Epic: in Virgil such personifications haunt the approach to the underworld[8] and Ovid in *Metamorphoses* descriptively expands the usage: *Invidia* (2.760-782); *Fames* (8.788-813); *Somnus* (11.592-615); and *Fama* (12.39-63). Valerius (2.116-122) includes a description of *Fama* which looks back to that of Virgil (*Aeneid* 4.173-188) and owes nothing to Ovid; and Statius, dutifully following Virgil, introduces *Fama* (6.552-554) and *Somnus* (10.340-356). In Lucan *Fortuna* is personified throughout as a divinity whom he regularly harangues and scolds, but otherwise he has no extended personification. It is Statius who takes up Ovid's lead: he constantly represents *Luctus, Pavor, Virtus*, etc.; he personifies Virgil's *Pietas* (11.457-496); his description of the House of Sleep (10.84-115, see on passage 31 below) is a masterpiece of this type of writing; and his representation of *Fama* (3.420-439 - passage 24 below) may be compared with its source and parallels (Appendix passage c below).

§27 The *Achilleid* was unfinished when the poet died. Indeed, only some 1,100 lines were written, the break coming in Book 2. In Book 1 Thetis, anxious for her son Achilles at the outbreak of the Trojan War, has hidden him, disguised as a girl (passage 32 below), on the island of Scyros amongst the daughters of Lycomedes. The youth

---

[8] *Aeneid* 6.274-280 - *Luctus, Curae, Morbi, Senectus, Metus, Fames, Egestas, Letum, Labor, Sopor, mala mentis Gaudia, Bellum, Discordia*.

makes love to one of them and is discovered by Ulixes
(Odysseus). At the sound of a trumpet Achilles is re-
vealed as a warrior (1.878-881):

> *illius intactae cecidere a pectore vestes,*
> *iam clipeus breviorque manu consumitur hasta*
> *(mira fides!) Ithacumque umeris excedere visus*
> *Aetolumque ducem.*[9]

And so Achilles is conscripted for the Trojan War. The
style of the *Achilleid* is generally less rhetorical and
less artificial than that of the *Thebaid*.

III GENERAL CHARACTERISTICS OF SILVER LATINITY

§28 A passion for terseness, a passion for novel modes of
expression, and a concentration of study upon poetic
authors were the three main influences at work in the
shaping of Silver latinity. Its chief features may be
summarised as follows:

1.   Widespread influx into prose of poetic elements
(with Virgil as a prime source). Tacitus, for example,
uses Virgilian words like *brevia* ('shoals'), and
adjectives like *indefessus* and *intemeratus* which both
Virgil and Ovid had used before him, while Seneca,
again with the example of poetry in mind, writes *senium*
for *senectus* and *Venus* for *amor*.

2.   Words in new meanings (e.g. *interim* = 'sometimes';
subinde = 'repeatedly'; *plerumque* = 'often'; *numerosus*
= 'numerous'; *familiaris* = 'usual'; *traducere* = 'expose
to ridicule'; *revolvere* = 'ponder'; *studere* = 'study').

3.   New formations (e.g. agent nouns in *-tor, -sor*;
abstracts in *-sus, -ura, -mentum*).

4.   The use of simple instead of compound verbs, which
had already been established as a feature in classical
poetry.

5.   The freer use of cases (e.g. dative of the agent
with a passive verb; ablative of separation without
preposition; ablative expressing duration of time; in-
strumental ablative even of persons).

6.   The use of the present and perfect subjunctive in
indirect speech after secondary tenses.

7.   The subjunctive of indefinite frequency.

8.   The use of *quamvis* and *quamquam* with the subjunctive

---

[9] Note the **vivid** *consumitur*; the spear is lost in his huge hand.

even when denoting facts.

9.   The interchange of *quin* and *quominus*.

10.   Fresh meanings of prepositions (e.g. *circa = de;
citra = sine*).

The points listed above apply generally to both poetry
and prose in the Silver Age, the two having by then
grown close together. Further information on
features of Silver latinity will be found in Furneaux's
introduction to his edition of Tacitus, *Annales* (1896),
and Summers' introductions to both *Select Letters of
Seneca* (1910) and Tacitus, *Histories* 3 (1904).

IV   GENERAL CHARACTERISTICS OF SILVER EPIC

§29 Straining after effect in a variety of ways is a notable
characteristic of Lucan and Statius. Valerius Flaccus
and Silius Italicus are not exempt from the tendency
but they do not display it to the same extent. The
subject may be divided under a number of headings.

Hyperbole

§30 Lucan is deeply imbued with the ranting exaggeration of
declamation as practised in the schools. Battles parti-
cularly brought out this tendency in him, as they did
too in Statius. Ovid may have been an important in-
fluence here, for there is a similar extravagance in
the battle scenes of the *Metamorphoses*. In fact, the
significance of Ovid for the development of Silver epic
as a whole - language, style, method and metre - must
not be ignored. In the naval battle fought during the
siege of Massilia (3.538-762) Lucan piles absurd horror
upon absurd horror.[10] The overdrawn account of Scaeva's
gallant fight (6.169-262) becomes laughable when Lucan
describes his vital parts as protected only by the spears
which stick fast when they reach his bones (194-195). In
Africa the description of a waterspout and a sandstorm
(9.457-471) exceeds the bounds of possibility; and Cato's
men, who have just escaped the region of serpents, are
- absurdly - gladdened by the realisation that it is
only lions with which they now have to contend (9.946f.).

§31 Statius can show similar lack of judgment. A mountain

---

[10] e.g. 3.635-646, the grisly dismemberment of Lycidas, which an
early commentator, Sulpitius, conjectured was the *carmen a se
compositum* (Tacitus, *Annals* 15.70) recited by Lucan as he bled
to death. If so, this might have drawn Milton to use the name
Lycidas for his drowned friend Edward King (*Notes and Queries*
201 (1956) 249; Dudley (1972) 111).

is so high that the stars rest upon it (Thebaid 2.32).[11]
The gruesome and the pathetic combine in a quite un-
classical way where Statius dwells in detail (Thebaid
5.596ff.) upon the savage mangling of a child's body
by a serpent; this seems even more strange from a poet
who is normally a lover of the beautiful but it seems
in conformity with the current taste for the horrific.
The appearance of the mutilated Oedipus is likewise
luridly presented (Thebaid 1.46-55). Again, Ennius
(Annales 519) had described a trumpet as completing of
itself a call prior to the decapitation of the trumpeter;
both Statius (Thebaid 11.53-56) and Silius Italicus (4.
173-174) borrow the incident. Statius' extravagance
can also be illustrated in his treatment of the story of
Hypsipyle, nurse of the Nemean king Lycurgus' infant son
Opheltes, and of the Lemnian women's murder of their hus-
bands (Thebaid 5.17-498); it forms an interesting contrast
to the restraint and delicacy of Valerius Flaccus' version
(2.311-427). Yet in battle descriptions (Book 6) even
Valerius is tempted into the infelicities typical of the
genre.

§32 If Silius Italicus is less strained in style, this may
arise from lack of imaginative power. Usually he is
straightforward and non-rhetorical but, like Valerius
and Statius, he sometimes pays Lucan the compliment of
imitation. The naval engagement off Syracuse (Book 14)
has many Lucanesque touches: a man is cut in two by a
ship's prow (481ff.); another has his wrists severed
by an axe and the ship speeds on with his hands still
sticking to the gunwale (489ff.); water seeps into
gaping wounds and then, expelled by the sobbing breath
of the wounded, pours back into the sea (550ff.). Simi-
larly, corpses bridge a river (15.767f.) and Lucan's
conceit (2.210ff.) in which the slain have no space to
fall recurs twice in Silius (4.553; 9.321). Though plain,
even flat at times, Silius' poetry can, nonetheless,
occasionally rise to a higher level: his invention of
two close friends, Marius and Caper of Praeneste, slain
together in battle (9.401ff.); the Carthaginian priest's
blue robe with jewels glittering on it (15.676f.); the
dramatic and vivid description of the meeting between
Syphax and Scipio early in the morning at the king's
palace, the lion cubs which are kept as pets being stroked
by the royal hand (16.229ff. - passage 22 below).

§33 Hyperbole is officially recognised as part of the orator's
resources (Quintilian 8.6.71) and is defined as "exag-
geration for the sake of effect". Its actual effect in

---

[11] cf. Valerius Flaccus 6.611 - the height of Caucasus considerably
increased by a snow-fall; a rare conceit for an otherwise
comparatively moderate poet.

the Silver epic poets not infrequently appears ludicrous.

Sententiae

§34 *Sententia* as a term employed by Roman rhetoricians and literary critics means a carefully polished thought. In post-Augustan times when rhetoric predominated the term came to be applied both to a striking thought, pointedly and thus memorably expressed, and to what would now be called an aphorism.[12]

§35 Lucan is full of *sententiae* and some examples are given below:

1.32 *alta sedent civilis vulnera dextrae* - 'the wounds inflicted by a fellow-citizen's hand go deep'.

1.81 *in se magna ruunt* - 'great things come crashing down on themselves'.

1.92 *nulla fides regni sociis* - 'there is no loyalty amongst sharers in tyranny'.

1.281 *semper nocuit differre paratis* - 'to delay is always harmful for those who are prepared'.

1.348-9 *arma tenenti / omnia dat qui iusta negat* - 'he who denies what is his due to the man who is armed yields him everything' (i.e. gives him an excuse for taking even more).

2.287 *sed quo fata trahunt virtus secura sequetur* - 'whither the Fates draw her Virtue will follow without fear' (a commonplace Stoic sentiment).

3.58 *nescit plebes ieiuna timere* - 'a hungry people does not know fear'.

4.704 *variam semper dant otia mentem* - 'idleness always creates an indecisive attitude'.

4.708 *qua stetit inde favet* - 'each man favours his own cause'.

5.260 *quidquid multis peccatur inultum est* - 'where it is many who do the wrong punishment is out of the question'.

8.260 *in dubiis tutum est inopem simulare tyranno* - 'in time of peril a prince finds safety in disguise as a poor man'.

9.211 *scire mori sors prima viris, sed proxima cogi* - 'the best fortune for men is to know when to die; the next

---

[12] W. H. Auden and L. Kronenberger (edd.), *The Faber Book of Aphorisms* (London, 1964) collects such maxims from many authors of different periods and backgrounds.

best is to have death forced upon them'.

10.407 *nulla fides pietasque viris qui castra sequuntur* - 'those who follow the camp have no loyalty, no sense of duty'.

§36 In contrast to Lucan, Statius works more by careful and erudite elaboration of the traditional epic material than by concise maxim and antithesis. The pithy aphorism (such as *nil falsum trepidis* (*Thebaid* 7.131) - 'the panic-stricken believe everything') is far rarer than in Lucan, but the *sententiae*, striking thoughts pointedly put, occur frequently:

Thebaid

1.322-3 *spes anxia mentem / extrahit et longo consumit gaudia voto* - 'anxious hope keeps his mind on edge and in far-reaching prayers he tastes the joys he desires' (on hope deferred).

1.547 *vivoque etiam pallescit in auro* - 'and even grows pale in the living gold' (of a Gorgon's severed head realistically represented on a golden cup).

1.620 *magnaque post lacrimas etiamnum gaudia pallent* - 'their gladness though great now that their grief is ended is wan and sickly' (of a crowd aghast over the body of a vampire which had preyed on local children).

1.623 *nequit iram explere potestas* - 'they can - and yet cannot - satisfy their wrath' (of the same crowd mangling the body in revenge).

4.94-5 *... iam laetus et integer artus, / ut primae strepuere tubae ...* - '(Tydeus) ... now blithe and re-stored in body, as soon as the first trumpets sounded (led forth his native troops) ...' (of Tydeus, his wounds healed, ready and eager for action - a vivid impression of dependable soldierliness conveyed in just a few words).

10.181 *haud laeti seque huc crevisse dolentes* - 'scarcely joyful and grieving that they have risen so high' (of men promoted to take the place of fallen leaders).

10.543 *immemores leti et tantum sua tela videntes* - 'un-mindful of death and with eyes for nothing except their own weapons' (of the invaders advancing with eyes fixed upon the walls).

11.446 *palluit amisso veniens in Tartara caelo* - 'he paled as he came to Hell after the loss of Heaven' (from the simile of Pluto's assumption of rule over the Underworld).

Achilleid

1.214 *vix stetit in ramis, et protinus arbor amatur* - 'scarcely has she alighted on the bough, but instantly the tree is dear to her' (of Thetis reassured that her son Achilles has been found a satisfactory haven on Scyros,

like a bird that has discovered a tree where her young
will be safe from cold and attack by snake or man).

§37 The low-keyed Valerius Flaccus usually hesitates to
interpose himself between the reader and the tale. He
uses few *sententiae* and the following list is perhaps
exhaustive:

1.30 *virtusque haud laeta tyranno* - 'valour, which hardly
delights a tyrant'.

1.76-7 *tu sola animos mentesque peruris, / gloria!* - 'you,
Fame, alone fire men's hearts and minds!' (cf. "fame is
the spur").

2.263-4 *stabilem quando optima facta / dant animum maior-
que piis audacia coeptis* - 'since good deeds give courage
and boldness is increased by righteous acts'.

4.158 *melior vulgi nam saepe voluntas* - 'for often the
ordinary people have greater kindliness'.

4.470 *miseris festina senectus* - 'old age which comes
quickly for the wretched'.

4.622 *saepe acri potior prudentia dextra* - 'wisdom is
often better than a vigorous right hand'.

4.744 *certa fides animis, idem quibus incidit hostis* -
'when men have met the same foe there is a sure bond of
loyalty amongst them in their hearts'.

5.536 *sceptri sic omnibus una cupido* - 'so all men share
the desire for power'.

7.227 *omnibus hunc potius communem animantibus orbem, /
communes et crede deos* - 'believe rather that this earth
is shared by all living creatures, and that the gods too
are shared'.

7.510 *questus semper Furor ultus amantum* - 'the Fury who
always avenges the complaints of lovers'.

§38 Silius Italicus, despite his general simplicity of style,
produces a few effective aphorisms:

3.145 *quantum etenim distant a morte silentia vitae* -
'how small is the difference between an obscure life and
death!'.

4.603-4 *explorant adversa viros, perque aspera duro /
nititur ad laudem virtus interrita clivo* - 'adversity
tests manhood, and courage strives to reach glory through
difficulties unterrified by the hard path'.

4.732 *pelle moras; brevis est magni fortuna favoris* -
'banish delay; short-lived is fortune's favour'.

5.100 *bellandum est astu; levior laus in duce dextrae* -
'war must be waged by craft; the right arm of a general
wins less fame'.

7.89 *rarae fumant felicibus arae* - 'when things go well
altars rarely smoke'.

7.55 *succensere nefas patriae* - 'to be angry against one's
country is a sin'.

8.95 *non umquam spem ponit amor* - 'love never abandons
hope'.

13.663 *ipsa quidem virtus sibimet pulcherrima merces* -
'virtue herself is her own noblest reward'.

Apostrophe and Moralising

§39 Apostrophe (a sudden turning aside from narrative to
address some person or object, absent or present) is a
device already found, though infrequently, in Homer
(e.g. *Iliad* 4.127f.). It became a mannerism of Hel-
lenistic poetry, providing dramatic variety and an
emotional or subjective atmosphere of intimacy.
Catullus uses it considerably (e.g. 4.13; 64.22 and 69;
68.93 and 105), Virgil sparingly but effectively, some-
times to enlist sympathy for a pathetic incident (e.g.
Aeneid 2.429ff. - the death of Panthus; 6.30f. - the
fall of Icarus), sometimes to add emotional impact in
a battle scene (e.g. 10.324ff., 390ff., 402f., 411 and
514), and sometimes to give variety to a catalogue (e.g.
7.684). Ovid employs it freely and Lucan incessantly
and lengthily (especially in Books 7 and 8). Statius
also makes regular use of it (e.g. *Thebaid* 3.99ff.;
6.481ff.; 11.574ff.).

§40 Moralising often accompanies apostrophe. An interesting
instance is provided by Lucan (4.799-824), which may be
analysed as follows:

799-804 Apostrophe to Curio.
805-806 Apostrophe to political leaders in general.
807-810 Moralising (destructive results of power seeking).
811-813 Apostrophe to Curio again.
814-824 More moralising (ambition and luxury).

§41 Since Valerius Flaccus tends, in the manner of earlier
epic, to avoid obtruding his personality, apostrophe (and
moralising) are not within his repertoire. The moralising
found in Lucan, Statius and Silius Italicus can to some
extent be ascribed to their interest in Stoicism; the
diatribe or harangue on moral issues was one of that
philosophy's standard features. Statius, for example, at
the start of the *Thebaid* (1.144-164), after recounting
the break between Oedipus' two sons, dilates - with an
added dash of apostrophe (155f.) - on what it meant to
be a king in remote and simple times, and on the poverty
of a kingdom for which the contenders were ready to kill
one another. Similarly Silius Italicus (11.28-54),
handling a trite theme, declaims against the wealth and

luxurious habits of the Capuans who were inclined to
side with the Carthaginians.

Erudition

§42 Learning was regarded as a necessary ingredient of poetry
in the Silver Age. The declaimers sought to impress by
elaborate concentration on detail and that attitude, like
their style, affected poetry. Thus Silver epic tends
to subordinate the whole to the parts, lavishing attention
on the learned "set-piece" digression. An excursus on
some abstruse topic or a general scholarly allusiveness
pleased the educated public; it flattered their own
level of culture and afforded evidence of the poet's
competence in his craft.

§43 Lucan is full of literary didacticism. He is fond of a
learned catalogue: when Caesar is withdrawing from Gaul
(1.392-465), there is a list of Gallic places and tribes
(see introductory note to passage 3 below); the age's
taste for the bizarre and ghoulish figures strongly in
the long section (6.434-569) on Thessalian witches;
Cato's presence in Africa provides an opportunity for
the poet to discourse (9.619-699) on the real and
legendary plagues of the region; he then turns (9.700-
838) to the local snakes, their bites and a list of their
victims, with particulars of the way each one dies. Geo-
graphy was a favourite and tempting subject: Lucan
introduces a disquisition concerning the geography
and mythological history of Thessaly (6.333-412); he
digresses, too, on the physical geography of Italy
(2.394-438). Valerius Flaccus gratuitously inserts
(4.711-732) an account of the Euxine (Black Sea), while
his catalogue of Scythians (6.33-162) is not unlike a
versified excerpt from some work on geography. Similarly,
Silius Italicus includes a lengthy passage (14.11-78) on
Sicily. Statius' detailed description (*Thebaid* 4.1-344)
of the seven champions banded together against Thebes is
at once a geographical and a mythological catalogue.
Mythology is this poet's forte; the reader's knowledge is
challenged by the diversity of allusive epithets applied,
for example, to Thebes (Aonian - 1.34; Echionian - 1.169
and 2.90; Ogygian - 1.173, 1.32 and 2.85; Sidonian - 3.656).
The poet's speculation (*Thebaid* 7.809-815) on the natural
causes which produced the chasm into which the augur
Amphiaraus disappears recalls the *Naturales Quaestiones* of
Seneca or the tone of Lucan when he enters into philo-
sophical or "scientific" discussion of natural phenomena
(e.g. 1.67ff.; 2.7ff.; 5.93ff.; 9.495ff.: 10.262ff.).
Compilations and treatises on a great range of subjects
from astronomy to zoology formed an important source for
Silver epic poets. That these were suitable subjects for
hexameter verse was also indicated by the traditions of
didactic poetry: in the Hellenistic period, for example,

Aratus' *Phaenomena* (translated into Latin more than once, including a version by Cicero, and extensively used by Virgil in *Georgics* 1) or the poems of Nicander (including the subject of snake bites and their cures); and in Latin literature Lucretius, Virgil's *Georgics* and Manilius.

In Summary

§44 The four poets represented in this volume would have had no difficulty in accepting "trained habit" as a definition of their art. The vocation of poetry meant close application to a body of knowledge which, in the form of rhetorical tropes and figures and all the trappings of traditional literary education (outlined by Quintilian), it was their task to deploy as imaginatively as possible. Cleverness, the poet's dexterity in the use of recognised resources, was part of the exercise. Expansion of detail was regular, even at the expense of proportion. The similes, for instance, are Hellenistic rather than Homeric, depicting the minute particulars of a scene or displaying the poet's command of mythological lore; they often extend to seven lines or more (though Valerius Flaccus, by contrast, keeps most of his similes to no more than four). There is a profuse vigour about Silver epic with its long *ekphraseis* and accumulation of special effects. It is all so different from Virgil. One might say that the difference between reading Silver epic and reading Virgil is like that between walking in a forest and walking in a park. But a forest is as much part of nature as a park; taste and sensibility differ from one age to another.

§45 Silver epic embodies a quality for which "romanticism" would be no misnomer. For romanticism is the natural successor to classicism whenever that reserved and controlled mode has run out of inspiration and lost its impetus. It may be found in Greek literature of the Hellenistic age as well as in the Silver age of Latin literature. There is a freer, more exuberantly imaginative style which includes within its ambit the bizarre and the supernatural, the sentimental and the pitiable.[13] Lucan's romanticism perhaps shows in his fascination with the horrific, the violence and cruelty of his battle scenes, his morbid interest in the supernatural; that of Valerius Flaccus in the tender charm of his treatment of

---

[13] It may be worth comparing the "Romantic Revival" of the late eighteenth and early nineteenth centuries, whose greater freedom of imagination included an appreciative interest in wild nature and inspiration from mediaeval literature and Gothic architecture. See M. H. Abrams, *The Mirror and the Lamp* (London and New York, 1953); Northrop Frye (ed.), *Romanticism Reconsidered* (New York, 1963); J. B. Halsted (ed.), *Romanticism* (Boston, 1965).

the love of Jason and Medea; that of Statius in his
sentimental attitude, which can reach real pathos, as
in the death of young Parthenopaeus - and the poet
was clearly fond of young people - at *Thebaid* 9.877ff.
(cf. passage 30 below):

> at puer infusus sociis in devia campi
> tollitur - heu simplex aetas! - moriensque iacentem
> flebat equum.

Silius, too, emulates Lucan's depiction of slaughter and can
show a pleasing touch of the romantic, as in the scene
where Syphax and Scipio meet (16.229ff. - passage 22
below; §32 above).

§46 Classicism is impersonal; the poet does not invite the
reader to look at *him*; he points and the more we follow
his pointing the less his personality obtrudes. By
contrast, Lucan starts from the word, from his interest
in the resources of expression, and moves to the thing.
In his similes, for example, the illustrative effect is
frequently dimmed through over-description; the poet's
self-consciousness comes between us and the object we
are invited to contemplate. Statius has observant eyes
but his imagination can freakishly assert itself and
lead to excess. Mannerism and romanticism go together
and appear when classicism has become exhausted. The
essence of classicism is discipline and simplicity. A
classical Greek temple was designed on chaste lines; so
was Greek tragedy; so, to a large extent, was the *Aeneid*.
Gothic architecture, on the other hand, has a romantic
exuberance, high-pointed arches, clustered columns,
extensive ornamental embellishment. Post-classical epic
exhibits a similar tendency to elaboration; classical
austerity had gone; we should be prepared for a dif-
ferent estimate of what is relevant or organic.

§47 Living to-day in an age of lyrical poetry we may well
find epic alien to us. We do not know what to make of
long poems. (How many still read *The Faerie Queene* of
Paradise Lost complete - and for pleasure?) The true
appreciation of epic requires an effort. Only by reading
through (in translation) the whole *corpus* of poetry re-
presented in this volume will it be possible to understand
the whole rambling edifice of each poem and set against it
the individual passages selected.

V   A NOTE ON METRE

§48 The hexameter of the Silver Latin epic poet looks back to
that of Ovid. As a metrician Ovid combined the highest
dexterity and smoothness with a lack of the harmonious

variation of rhythms which is the mark of Virgil.[14]
His hexameters show far fewer examples of elision than
Virgil's, and they avoid the various irregularities and
departures from the usual which are common in Virgil.
They tend to scan by accent more than those of the
Aeneid, i.e. there is a greater proportion of feet which
commence with a syllable bearing a natural stress. Train-
ing and practice lie behind this; it is very much a
matter of rules. To try to emulate the rich, subtle and
ever changing texture and pattern of Virgil's verse is
quite a different matter. All subsequent writers of
hexameters, even those who otherwise clearly admire and
imitate Virgil, are more or less Ovidian in their handling
of the medium.

---

[14] A similar distinction might be drawn between Pope and Milton.

SELECT BIBLIOGRAPHY

(references in the Introduction and Notes are made simply by author's
name and date)

Ahl, F. M.:   *Lucan* (Cornell, 1976).

Albrecht, M. von: 'Lucan und die epische Tradition' in
                               Lucain, Fondation Hardt Entretiens
                               15 (Geneva, 1968) 267-308.

Austin, R. G. (ed.):   *Virgil*, Aeneid I (Oxford, 1971).
                               Virgil, Aeneid II (Oxford, 1964).
                               Virgil, Aeneid IV (Oxford, 1955).
                               Virgil, Aeneid VI (Oxford, 1977).

Aymard, J.:   *Quelques Séries de Comparaisons chez
                               Lucain* (Montpellier, 1951).

Bardon, H.:   "Le Goût à l'Époque des Flaviens",
                               Latomus 21 (1962) 732-748.

Barratt, P. (ed.):   *Lucan V : a Commentary* (Amsterdam, 1979).

Bonner, S. F.:   *Roman Declamation in the late Republic
                               and early Empire* (Liverpool, 1949).
                               "Lucan and the Declamation Schools",
                               American Journal of Philology 87
                               (1966) 257-289.

Brisset, J.:   *Les Idées politiques de Lucain* (Paris, 1964).

Burck, E.:   *Vom Römischen Manierismus* (Darmstadt, 1971).

Burgess, F. J.:   "*Pietas* in Virgil and Statius", *Proceedings
                               of the Virgil Society* 11 (1971) 48-61.

Butler, H. E.:   *Post-Augustan Poetry* (Oxford, 1909).

Charlesworth, M. P.:   "The Virtues of a Roman Emperor", *Proceedings
                               of the British Academy* 23 (1937) 105-133.

Dilke, O. A. W.:   *Statius,* Achilleid (Cambridge, 1954).
                               Lucan VII (Cambridge, 1960, reprinted by
                               Bristol Classical Press, 1978).

Dudley, D. R. (ed.):   *Neronians and Flavians* (London, 1972).

Due, O. S.:   "An essay on Lucan", *Classica et Mediaevalia*
                               23 (1962) 68-132.

Fitch, J. G.:   "Aspects of Valerius Flaccus' use of Similes", *Transactions of the American Philological Association* 106 (1976) 113-124.

Fordyce, C. J. (ed.):   *Catullus: A Commentary* (Oxford, 1961).

Fortgens, H. W. (ed.):   *Statius,* Thebaid *VI,* 1-295 (Zutphen, 1934).

Freidrich, W. -H.:   "Cato, Caesar und Fortuna bei Lucan", *Hermes* 73 (1938) 391-423.
"Episches Unwetter" *in Festschrift Bruno Snell* (Munich, 1956) 77-87.

Garson, R. W.:   "The Hylas Episode in Valerius Flaccus' *Argonautica*", Classical Quarterly 13 (1963) 260-267.
"Some Critical Observations on Valerius Flaccus' *Argonautica*", *Classical Quarterly* 14 (1964) 267-279 and 15 (1965) 104-120.

Getty, R. J.:   *Lucan I* (Cambridge, 1955 - 2nd ed.).

Gossage, A. J.:   "Statius" in Dudley (1972) 184-235.

Gransden, K. W. (ed.):   *Virgil,* Aeneid *VIII* (Cambridge, 1976).

Grimal, P.:   "L'Éloque de Néron au début de la **Pharsale**", *Revue des Études Latines* 38 (1960) 296-305.

Hardie, A.:   *Statius and the Silvae* (Liverpool, 1983).

Haskins, C. E. and
  Heitland, W. E. (edd.):   *Lucani* Pharsalia (London, 1887).

Hauser, A.:   *Mannerism* (London, 1965).

Helm, R.:   "Lucanus", *Lustrum* I (1956) 163-128.

Hollis, A. S. (ed.):   *Ovid,* Metamorphoses *VIII* (Oxford, 1970).

Hull, K. W. D.:   "The Hero-concept in Valerius Flaccus' *Argonautica*" in *Studies in Latin Literature and Roman History, Collection Latomus* 164 (Brussels, 1979) 379-409.

Jenkinson, J. R.:   "Sarcasm in Lucan 1 33-66", *Classical Review* 24 (1974) 8-9.

Kenney, E. J. and
  Clausen, W. V. (edd.):   *The Cambridge History of Classical Literature* (Cambridge, 1982).

Kytzler, B.:   "Gleichnisgruppen in der *Thebais* des Statius", *Wiener Studien* 75 (1962) 141-160.
"Der Bittgang der argivischen Frauen", *Der altsprachliche Unterricht* 2 (1968) 50-61.

Langen, P. (ed.):   *Valerii Flacci Argonauticorum Libri VIII*
(Berlin, 1897).

Legras, L.:   *Étude sur la Thébaide de Stace* (Paris, 1905).

Lemaire, N. E. (ed.):   *Silii Italici Punicorum Libri XII* (Paris, 1823).

Lepper, F. A.:   "Some Reflections on the *Quinquennium Neronis*", *Journal of Roman Studies* 47 (1957) 95-103.

Martindale, C. A.:   "Paradox, Hyperbole and Literary Novelty in Lucan's *de Bello Civili*", *Bulletin of the Institute of Classical Studies* 23 (1976) 45-54.

Mayer, R. (ed.):   *Lucan, Civil War VIII* (Warminster, 1981).

Momigliano, A.:   "Literary Chronology of the Neronian Age", *Classical Quarterly* 38 (1944) 96-100.

Morford, M. P. O.:   *The Poet Lucan* (Oxford, 1967).

Mulder, H. M. (ed.):   *P. Papinii Statii Thebaidos Liber II* (Groningen, 1954).

Narducci, E.:   "Lucan I 52-695", *Maia* 26 (1974) 97-110.

Nisard, D.:   *Etudes sur les Poètes latines de la Décadence* (Paris, 1849 - 2nd ed.).

Perkins, J.:   "An Aspect of the Style of Valerius Flaccus' *Argonautica*", *Phoenix* 28 (1974) 290-313.

Postgate, J. P. (ed.):   *Lucan VIII* (Cambridge, 1917).

Ruperti, G. A. (ed.):   *Silius Italicus, Punica* (Göttingen, 1795).

Rutz, W. (ed.):   *Lucan, Wege der Forschung* 235 (Darmstadt, 1970).

Schetter, W.:   *Untersuchungen zur epischen Kunst des Statius* (Wiesbaden, 1960).

Snijder, H. (ed.):   *P. Papinius Statius*, Thebaid *III* (Amsterdam, 1968).

Strand, J.:   *Notes on Valerius Flaccus'* Argonautica (Göteborg-Stockholm, 1972).

Summers, W. C.:   *A Study of the* Argonautica *of Valerius Flaccus* (Cambridge, 1894).

Taylor, L. R.:   *The Divinity of the Roman Emperor* (Middletown, Connecticut, 1931).

Vessey, D.:   *Statius and the* Thebaid (Cambridge, 1973).

Warmington, E. H.:   *Remains of Old Latin*, Loeb Classical Library,
                                4 vols. (London and Harvard, 1957).

Williams, G. W.:   *Tradition and Originality in Roman Poetry*
                                (Oxford, 1968).
                                *Change and Decline: Roman Literature in the
                                Early Empire* (Berkeley and Los Angeles,
                                1978).

Williams, R. D. (ed.):   *Statius* Thebaid *X* (Leyden, 1972).

Winterbottom, M.:   *Roman Declamation* (Bristol Classical
                                Press, 1979).

LUCAN
Passages 1–7

1. INVOCATION TO NERO
(Lucan 1.33 – 66)

quod si non aliam venturo fata Neroni
invenere viam magnoque aeterna parantur
regna deis caelumque suo servire Tonanti   35
non nisi saevorum potuit post bella gigantum,
iam nihil, o superi, querimur; scelera ista nefasque
hac mercede placent; diros Pharsalia campos
inpleat et Poeni saturentur sanguine manes;
ultima funesta concurrant proelia Munda;   40
his, Caesar, Perusina fames Mutinaeque labores
accedant fatis et quas premit aspera classes
Leucas et ardenti servilia bella sub Aetna:
multum Roma tamen debet civilibus armis,
quod tibi res acta est. te, cum statione peracta   45
astra petes serus, praelati regia caeli
excipiet gaudente polo; seu sceptra tenere,
seu te flammigeros Phoebi conscendere currus,
telluremque nihil mutato sole timentem
igne vago lustrare iuvet, tibi numine ab omni   50
cedetur, iurisque tui natura relinquet,
quis deus esse velis, ubi regnum ponere mundi.
sed neque in Arctoo sedem tibi legeris orbe,
nec polus aversi calidus qua vergitur Austri,
unde tuam videas obliquo sidere Romam.   55
aetheris inmensi partem si presseris unam,
sentiet axis onus. librati pondera caeli
orbe tene medio; pars aetheris illa sereni
tota vacet, nullaeque obstent a Caesare nubes.
tum genus humanum positis sibi consulat armis,   60
inque vicem gens omnis amet; pax missa per orbem
ferrea belligeri conpescat limina Iani.
sed mihi iam numen; nec, si te pectore vates
accipio, Cirrhaea velim secreta moventem
sollicitare deum Bacchumque avertere Nysa: 65
tu satis ad vires Romana in carmina dandas.

1

2. PRODIGIES
(Lucan 1. 524 - 549)

superique minaces
prodigiis terras inplerunt, aethera, pontum.   525
ignota obscurae viderunt sidera noctes
ardentemque polum flammis caeloque volantes
obliquas per inane faces crinemque timendi
sideris et terris mutantem regna cometen.
fulgura fallaci micuerunt crebra sereno,   530
et varias ignis denso dedit aere formas,
nunc iaculum longo, nunc sparso lumine lampas.
emicuit caelo tacitum sine nubibus ullis
fulmen et Arctois rapiens de partibus ignem
percussit Latiare caput, stellaeque minores   535
per vacuum solitae noctis decurrere tempus
in medium venere diem, cornuque coacto
iam Phoebe toto fratrem cum redderet orbe,
terrarum subita percussa expalluit umbra.
ipse caput medio Titan cum ferret Olympo,   540
condidit ardentes atra caligine currus
involvitque orbem tenebris gentesque coegit
desperare diem; qualem fugiente per ortus
sole Thyesteae noctem duxere Mycenae.
ora ferox Siculae laxavit Mulciber Aetnae   545
nec tulit in caelum flammas, sed vertice prono
ignis in Hesperium cecidit latus.   atra Charybdis
sanguineum fundo torsit mare.   flebile saevi
latravere canes.

3. THE DRUIDS' GROVE
(Lucan 3. 399 - 452)

lucus erat longo numquam violatus ab aevo,
obscurum cingens conexis aera ramis   400
et gelidas alte summotis solibus umbras.
hunc non ruricolae Panes nemorumque potentes
silvani Nymphaeque tenent, sed barbara ritu
sacra deum; structae diris altaribus arae,
omnisque humanis lustrata cruoribus arbor   405
siqua fidem meruit superos mirata vetustas,
illis et volucres metuunt insistere ramis
et lustris recubare ferae; nec ventus in illas
incubuit silvas excussaque nubibus atris
fulgura; non ulli frondem praebentibus aurae   410
arboribus suus horror inest.   tum plurima nigris
fontibus unda cadit, simulacraque maesta deorum
arte carent caesisque extant informia truncis.
ipse situs putrique facit iam robore pallor

attonitos; non volgatis sacrata figuris 415
numina sic metuunt: tantum terroribus addit,
quos timeant, non nosse deos.   iam fama ferebat
saepe cavas motu terrae mugire cavernas,
et procumbentes iterum consurgere taxos,
et non ardentis fulgere incendia silvae, 420
roboraque amplexos circumfluxisse dracones.
non illum cultu populi propiore frequentant
sed cessere deis.   medio cum Phoebus in axe est
aut caelum nox atra tenet, pavet ipse sacerdos
accessus dominumque timet deprendere luci. 425
hanc iubet inmisso silvam procumbere ferro;
nam vicina operi belloque intacta priore
inter nudatos stabat densissima montes.
sed fortes tremuere manus, motique verenda
maiestate loci, si robora sacra ferirent, 430
in sua credebant redituras membra secures.
inplicitas magno Caesar torpore cohortes
ut vidit, primus raptam librare bipennem
ausus et aeriam ferro proscindere quercum
effatur merso violata in robora ferro: 435
'iam ne quis vestrum dubitet subvertere silvam,
credite me fecisse nefas.'   tum paruit omnis
imperiis non sublato secura pavore
turba, sed expensa superorum et Caesaris ira.
procumbunt orni, nodosa inpellitur ilex, 440
silvaque Dodones et fluctibus aptior alnus
et non plebeios luctus testata cupressus
tum primum posuere comas et fronde carentes
admisere diem, propulsaque robore denso
sustinuit se silva cadens.   gemuere videntes 445
Gallorum populi; muris sed clausa iuventus
exultat; quis enim laesos inpune putaret
esse deos?   servat multos fortuna nocentes,
et tantum miseris irasci numina possunt.
utque satis caesi nemoris, quaesita per agros 450
plaustra ferunt, curvoque soli cessantis aratro
agricolae raptis annum flevere iuvencis.

—

4. FRENZY OF THE PROPHETESS
(Lucan 5. 169 – 197)

bacchatur demens aliena per antrum *demo*
colla ferens, vittasque dei Phoebeaque serta 170
ergo erectis discussa comis per inania templi *discutio*
anceps ancipiti cervice rotat spargitque vaganti *spargo*
obstantes tripodas magnoque exaestuat igne
iratum te, Phoebe, ferens.   nec verbere solo
uteris et stimulos flammasque in viscera mergis: *mergo* 175

accipit et frenos, nec tantum prodere vati
quantum scire licet.   venit aetas omnis in unam

congero congeriem, miserumque premunt tot saecula pectus,
tanta patet rerum series, atque omne futurum

nitor nititur in lucem, vocemque petentia fata   180

luctor luctantur; non prima dies, non ultima mundi,
non modus Oceani, numerus non derat harenae.   *cto*
qualis in Euboico vates Cumana recessu, *recedo*

indignor indignata suum multis servire furorem
gentibus, ex tanta fatorum strage superba   185

excerpo excerpsit Romana manu, sic plena laborat
Phemonoe Phoebo, dum te, consultor operti
Castalia tellure dei, vix invenit, Appi,

quaero inter fata diu quaerens tam magna latentem. *lateo*
spumea tunc primum rabies vaesana per ora   190
effluit et gemitus et anhelo clara meatu
murmura, tum maestus vastis ululatus in antris
extremaeque sonant domita iam virgine voces:
'effugis ingentes, tanti discriminis expers,

mino bellorum, Romane, minas, solusque quietem   195
Euboici vasta lateris convalle tenebis.'

supprimo cetera suppressit faucesque obstruxit Apollo.

5. AMYCLAS

(Lucan 5. 504 – 596)

solverat armorum fessas nox languida curas,
parva quies miseris, in quorum pectora somno   505
dat vires fortuna minor; iam castra silebant,
tertia iam vigiles commoverat hora secundos;
Caesar sollicito per vasta silentia gressu
vix famulis audenda parat, cunctisque relictis
sola placet Fortuna comes.   tentoria postquam   510
egressus vigilum somno cedentia membra
transsiluit questus tacite, quod fallere posset,
litora curva legit primisque invenit in undis
rupibus exesis haerentem fune carinam.
rectorem dominumque ratis secura tenebat   515
haud procul inde domus, non ullo robore fulta
sed sterili iunco cannaque intexta palustri
et latus inversa nudum munita phaselo.
haec Caesar bis terque manu quassantia tectum
limina commovit.   molli consurgit Amyclas,   520
quem dabat alga, toro. 'quisnam mea naufragus,' inquit,
'tecta petit? aut quem nostrae fortuna coegit
auxilium sperare casae?'   sic fatus ab alto
aggere iam tepidae sublato fune favillae
scintillam tenuem commotos pavit in ignes,   525
securus belli; praedam civilibus armis

scit non esse casas. o vitae tuta facultas
pauperis angustique lares! o munera nondum
intellecta deum! quibus hoc contingere templis
aut potuit muris, nullo trepidare tumultu   530
Caesarea pulsante manu? tum poste recluso
dux ait: 'expecta votis maiora modestis
spesque tuas laxa, iuvenis: si iussa secutus
me vehis Hesperiam, non ultra cuncta carinae
debebis manibusque importunamve fereris
pauperiem deflens inopem duxisse senectam.   535
ne cessa praebere deo tua fata volenti
angustos opibus subitis inplere poenates.'
sic fatur, quamquam plebeio tectus amictu,
indocilis privata loqui. tum pauper Amyclas:
'multa quidem prohibent nocturno credere ponto;   540
nam sol non rutilas deduxit in aequora nubes
concordesque tulit radios: Noton altera Phoebi,
altera pars Borean diducta luce vocabat.
orbe quoque exhaustus medio languensque recessit
spectantes oculos infirmo lumine passus.   545
lunaque non gracili surrexit lucida cornu
aut orbis medii puros exesa recessus,
nec duxit recto tenuata cacumina cornu,
ventorumque notam rubuit; tum lurida pallens
ora tulit voltu sub nubem tristis ituro.   550
sed mihi nec motus nemorum nec litoris ictus
nec placet incertus qui provocat aequora delphin,
aut siccum quod mergus amat, quodque ausa volare
ardea sublimis pinnae confisa natanti,
quodque caput spargens undis, velut occupet imbrem,
instabili gressu metitur litora cornix.   556
sed si magnarum poscunt discrimina rerum,
haud dubitem praebere manus: vel litora tangam
iussa, vel hoc potius pelagus flatusque negabunt.'
haec fatur solvensque ratem dat carbasa ventis,   560
ad quorum motus non solum lapsa per altum
aera dispersos traxere cadentia sulcos
sidera, sed summis etiam quae fixa tenentur
astra polis sunt visa quati. niger inficit horror
terga maris, longo per multa volumina tractu   565
aestuat unda minax, flatusque incerta futuri
turbida testantur conceptos aequora ventos.
tunc rector trepidae fatur ratis: 'aspice, saevum
quanta paret pelagus; Zephyros intendat an Austros,
incertum est: puppim dubius ferit undique pontus. 570
nubibus et caelo Notus est; si murmura ponti
consulimus, Cori veniet mare. gurgite tanto
nec ratis Hesperias tanget nec naufragus oras.
desperare viam et vetitos convertere cursus
sola salus. liceat vexata litora puppe   575
prendere, ne longe nimium sit proxima tellus.'

fisus cuncta sibi cessura pericula Caesar,
'sperne minas', inquit, 'pelagi ventoque furenti
trade sinum.   Italiam si caelo auctore recusas,
me pete.   sola tibi causa est haec iusta timoris,   580
vectorem non nosse tuum, quem numina numquam
destituunt, de quo male tunc fortuna meretur,
cum post vota venit.   medias perrumpe procellas
tutela secure mea.   caeli iste fretique,
non puppis nostrae, labor est: hanc Caesare pressam   585
a fluctu defendet onus.   nec longa furori
ventorum saevo dabitur mora: proderit undis
ista ratis.   ne flecte manum, fuge proxima velis
litora: tum Calabro portu te crede potitum,
cum iam non poterit puppi nostraeque saluti   590
altera terra dari.   quid tanta strage paretur,
ignoras: quaerit pelagi caelique tumultu,
quod praestet Fortuna mihi.'   non plura locuto
avolsit laceros percussa puppe rudentes
turbo rapax fragilemque super volitantia malum   595
vela tulit; sonuit victis conpagibus alnus.

Tuesday

6. POMPEY'S NEGLECTED CORPSE
(Lucan 8. 698 – 711)

litora Pompeium feriunt, truncusque vadosis
huc illuc iactatur aquis.   adeone molesta
totum cura fuit socero servare cadaver?   700
hac Fortuna fide Magni tam prospera fata
pertulit, hac illum summo de culmine rerum
morte petit cladesque omnes exegit in uno
saeva die, quibus inmunes tot praestitit annos,
Pompeiusque fuit, qui numquam mixta videret (subj) 705
laeta malis, felix nullo turbante deorum
et nullo parcente miser; semel inpulit illum
dilata Fortuna manu.   pulsatur harenis,
carpitur in scopulis hausto per volnera fluctu,
ludibrium pelagi, nullaque manente figura   710
una nota est Magno capitis iactura revolsi.

relative clause of characteristic

7. POMPEY DEAD ✓
(Lucan 9. 1 – 18)

at non in Pharia manes iacuere favilla,
nec cinis exiguus tantam conpescuit umbram:
prosiluit busto semustaque membra relinquens
degeneremque rogum sequitur convexa Tonantis.

but he did not remain, lying in the Egyptian embers, nor are the meager ashes imprisoned in such a great ghost, he jumps up from the grave & leaves behind half burnt limbs, and the well-rounded thunder accompanies an inferior funeral pyre.

qua niger astriferis conectitur axibus aer   5
quodque patet terras inter lunaeque meatus,
semidei manes habitant, quos ignea virtus
innocuos vita patientes aetheris imi
fecit, et aeternos animam collegit in orbes:
non illuc auro positi nec ture sepulti   10
perveniunt.   illic postquam se lumine vero
inplevit, stellasque vagas miratus et astra
fixa polis, vidit quanta sub nocte iaceret
nostra dies, risitque sui ludibria trunci.
hinc super Emathiae campos et signa cruenti   15
Caesaris ac sparsas volitavit in aequore classes,
et scelerum vindex in sancto pectore Bruti
sedit et invicti posuit se mente Catonis.

VALERIUS FLACCUS
Passages 8–16

8. STORM AT SEA
(Valerius Flaccus 1. 608 – 642)

at cuncti fremere intus et aequora venti
poscere. tum validam contorto turbine portam
impulit Hippotades. fundunt se carcere laeti   610
Thraces equi Zephyrusque et nocti concolor alas
nimborum cum prole Notus crinemque procellis
hispidus et multa flavus caput Eurus harena;
induxere hiemem raucoque ad litora tractu
unanimi freta curva ferunt nec sola Tridentis   615
regna movent; vasto pariter ruit igneus aether
cum tonitru piceoque premit nox omnia caelo.
excussi manibus remi conversaque frontem
puppis in obliquum resonos latus accipit ictus;
vela super tremulum subitus volitantia malum   620
turbo rapit. qui tum Minyis trepidantibus horror,
cum picei fulsere poli pavidamque coruscae
ante ratem cecidere faces, antemnaque laevo
prona dehiscentem cornu cum sustulit undam!
non hiemem missosque putant consurgere ventos   625
ignari, sed tale fretum. tum murmure maesto
'hoc erat inlicitas temerare rudentibus undas
quod nostri timuere patres. vix litore puppem
solvimus, et quanto fremitu se sustulit Aegon!
hocine Cyaneae concurrunt aequore cautes?   630
tristius an miseris superest mare? linquite, terrae,
spem pelagi sacrosque iterum seponite fluctus.'
haec iterant segni flentes occumbere leto.
magnanimus spectat pharetras et inutile robur
Amphitryoniades; miscent suprema paventes   635
verba alii iunguntque manus atque ora fatigant
aspectu in misero toti, cum protinus alnus
solvitur et vasto puppis mare sorbet hiatu.
illam huc atque illuc nunc torquens verberat Eurus;
nunc strideus Zephyris aufert Notus; undique fervent 640
aequora, cum subitus trifida Neptunus in hasta
caeruleum fundo caput extulit.

9

the dreadful
hour had
been raised,
now turning
themselves
to the heavens
in order to
carry off the
beauty & at
the same time
the mountains
& the place
from the eyes
and to see
the painful
darkness
surrounded.

9. NIGHT SCENE AT SEA
(Valerius Flaccus 2. 38 – 58)

auxerat hora metus, iam se vertentis Olympi
ut faciem raptosque simul montesque locosque
ex oculis circumque graves videre tenebras.   40
ipsa quies rerum mundique silentia terrent
astraque et effusis stellatus crinibus aether.
ac velut ignota captus regione viarum
noctivagum qui carpit iter non aure quiescit,
non oculis, noctisque metus niger auget utrimque   45
campus et occurrens umbris maioribus arbor,
haud aliter trepidare viri.   sed pectora firmans
Hagniades, 'non hanc,' inquit, 'sine numine pinum
derigimus, nec me tantum Tritonia cursus
erudiit; saepe ipsa manu dignata carinam est.   50
an non experti, subitus cum luce fugata
horruit imbre dies? quantis, pro Iuppiter, austris
restitimus! quanta quotiens et Palladis arte
incassum decimae cecidit tumor arduus undae!
quin agite, o socii; micat immutabile caelum   55
puraque nec gravido surrexit Cynthia cornu,
nullus in ore rubor, certusque ad talia Titan
integer in fluctus et in uno decidit auro.

10. AEETES' PALACE
(Valerius Flaccus 5. 416 – 454)

nec minus hinc varia dux laetus imagine templi
ad geminas fert ora fores cunabula gentis
Colchidos hic ortusque tuens; ut prima Sesostris
intulerit rex bella Getis, ut clade suorum
territus hos Thebas patriumque reducat ad amnem,   420
Phasidis hos imponat agris Colchosque vocari
imperet: Arsinoen illi tepidaeque requirunt
otia laeta Phari pinguemque sine imbribus annum,
et iam Sarmaticis permutant carbasa bracis.
barbarus in patriis sectatur montibus Aean   425
Phasis amore furens: pavidas iacit illa pharetras
virgineo turbata metu, discursibus et iam
deficit, ac volucri victam deus alligat unda.
flebant populeae iuvenem Phaethonta sorores,
ater et Eridani trepidum globus ibat in amnem;   430
at iuga vix Tethys sparsumque recolligit axem
et formidantem patrios Pyroenta dolores.
aurea quin etiam praesaga Mulciber arte
vellera venturosque olim caelarat Achivos.
texitur Argoa pinus Pagasaea securi,   435
ipse subit nudaque vocat dux agmina dextra.

iamque eadem remos, eadem dea flectit habenas;
exoritur notus et toto ratis una profundo
cernitur; Odrysio gaudebant carmine phocae.
apparent trepidi per Phasidis ostia Colchi   440
clamantemque procul linquens regina parentem.
urbs erat hinc contra gemino circumflua ponto,
ludus ubi et cantus taeda pernocte iugales
regalique toro laetus gener: ille priorem
deserit; ultrices spectant a culmine Dirae.   445
deficit in thalamis turbataque paelice coniunx
pallam et gemmiferae donum exitiale coronae
apparat ante omnes secum dequesta labores.
munere quo patrias paelex ornatur ad aras
infelix; et iam rutilis correpta venenis   450
implicat igne domus. haec tum miracula Colchis
struxerat Ignipotens nondum noscentibus, ille
quis labor, aligeris aut quae secet anguibus auras
caede madens: odere tamen visusque reflectunt.

11. MEDEA'S DREAM
(Valerius Flaccus 5. 329 – 342)

[teorum]

forte deum variis per noctem territa monstris,
senserat ut pulsas tandem Medea tenebras,   330
rapta toris primi iubar ad placabile Phoebi   (apostrophe)
ibat et horrendas lustrantia flumina noctes.
namque soporatos tacitis in sedibus artus
dum premit alta quies nullaeque in virgine curae,
visa pavens castis Hecates excedere lucis;   335
dumque pii petit ora patris, stetit arduus inter [Sto]
pontus et ingenti circum stupefacta profundo,
fratre tamen conante sequi; mox stare paventes (Indirect statement)
viderat intenta pueros nece seque trementum
spargere caede manus et lumina rumpere fletu.   340
his turbata minis fluvios ripamque petebat
Phasidis aequali Scythidum comitante caterva.

12. MEDEA ON THE CITY WALLS
(Valerius Flaccus 6.575 – 601)

ecce autem muris residens Medea paternis   575
singula dum magni lustrat certamina belli
atque hos ipsa procul densa in caligine reges
agnoscit quaeritque alios, Iunone magistra
conspicit Aesonium longe caput, ac simul acres
huc oculos sensusque refert animumque faventem,   580
nunc quo se raperet, nunc quo diversus abiret, (Indirect questions)
Subj   Subj

12

imperfect
because its
happening in the
epic past, historic
present

ante videns, quotque unus equos, quot funderet arma, *subj.*
errrantes.que.viros quam densis sisteret hastis.
quaque iterum tacito sparsit vaga lumina vultu
aut fratris quaerens aut pacti coniugis arma,   585
saevus ibi miserae solusque occurrit Iason.
tunc his germanam adgreditur, ceu nescia, dictis:
'quis, precor, hic, toto iamdudum fervere campo
quem tueor quemque ipsa vides? nam te quoque tali
attonitam virtute reor.' contra aspera Iuno   590
reddit agens stimulis ac diris fraudibus urget. *fraus*
'ipsum,' ait,' 'Aesoniden cernis, soror, aequore tanto
debita cognati repetit qui vellera Phrixi,
nec nunc laude prior generis nec sanguine quisquam.
aspicis, ut Minyas inter proceresque Cytaeos   595
emicet effulgens quantisque insultet acervis?
et iam vela dabit, iam litora nostra relinquet,
Thessaliae felicis opes dilectaque Phrixo
rura petens. eat atque utinam superetque labores!'
tantum effata magis campis intendere suadet,   600
dum datur, ardentesque viri percurrere pugnas.

13. MEDEA'S THOUGHTS OF JASON
(Valerius Flaccus 6.752 - 760)

nox simul astriferas profert optabilis umbras;
et cadit extemplo belli fragor aegraque muris
degreditur longum virgo perpessa timorem.
ut fera Nyctelii paulum per sacra resistunt,   755
mox rapuere deum iam iam in quodcumque paratae
Thyiades, haud alio remeat Medea tumultu,
atque inter Graiumque acies patriasque phalangas
semper inexpletis agnoscit Iasona curis
armaque quique cava superest de casside vultus.   760

14. MEDEA'S SLEEPLESS NIGHT
(Valerius Flaccus 7.1 - 25)

te quoque Thessalico iam serus ab hospite vesper
dividit et iam te tua gaudia, virgo, relinquunt,
noxque ruit soli veniens non mitis amanti.
ergo ubi cunctatis extremo in limine plantis
contigit aegra toros et mens incensa tenebris,   5
vertere tunc varios per longa insomnia questus
nec pereat quo scire malo; tandemque fateri
ausa sibi paulum medio sic fata dolore est:
'nunc ego quo casu vel quo sic pervigil usque
ipsa volens errore trahor? non haec mihi certe   10

nox erat ante tuos, iuvenis fortissime, vultus.
quos ego cur iterum demens iterumque recordor
tam magno discreta mari? quid in hospite solo
mens mihi? cognati potius iam vellera Phrixi
accipiat, quae sola petit quaeque una laborum   15
causa viro.   nam quando domos has ille reviset?
aut meus Haemonias quando pater ibit ad urbes?
felices, mediis qui se dare fluctibus ausi
nec tantas timuere vias talemque secuti
huc qui deinde virum: sed, sit quoque talis, abito.'   20
tum iactata toro totumque experta cubile
ecce videt tenui candescere limen Eoo,
nec minus insomnem lux orta refecit amantem,
quam cum languentes levis erigit imber aristas
grataque iam fessis descendunt flamina remis.   25

15. THE PERFIDIOUS AEETES
(Valerius Flaccus 7.78 - 81)

filia prima trucis vocem mirata tyranni
haesit et ad iuvenem pallentia rettulit ora
contremuitque metu, ne nescius audeat hospes   80
seque miser ne posse putet.

the first daughter, amazed by the voice of the savage tyrant, and she returns to the young man, growing pale at his adoration, & she trembled w/ fear, lest the stranger, in ignorance, dare, and miserable, believe he is not able. hesitates

16. CONFLICT OF FEELINGS
(Valerius Flaccus 7.103 - 126)

at trepida et medios inter deserta parentes
virgo silet, nec fixa solo servare parumper
lumina nec potuit maestos non flectere vultus,   105
respexitque fores et adhuc invenit euntem;
visus et heu miserae tunc pulchrior hospes amanti
discedens; tales umeros, ea terga relinquit.
illa domum atque ipsos paulum procedere postes
optat, at ardentes tenet intra limina gressus.   110
qualis ubi extremas Io vaga sentit harenas
fertque refertque pedem, tumido quam cogit Erinys
ire mari Phariaeque vocant trans aequora matres:
circuit haud aliter foribusque impendet apertis,
an melior Minyas revocet pater; oraque quaerens   115
hospitis aut solo maeret defecta cubili
aut venit in carae gremium refugitque sororis
atque loqui conata silet; rursusque recedens
quaerit, ut Aeaeis hospes consederit oris
Phrixus, ut aligeri Circen rapuere dracones.   120
tum comitum visu fruitur miseranda suarum
implerique nequit; subitoque parentibus haeret

blandior et patriae circumfert oscula dextrae.
sic adsueta toris et mensae dulcis erili
aegra nova iam peste canis rabieque futura ,   125
ante fugam totos lustrat queribunda penates.

SILIUS ITALICUS
Passages 17–22

17. THE RIVER TICINUS
(Silius Italicus 4.81 – 87)

haec ait atque agmen Ticini flectit ad undas.
caeruleas Ticinus aquas et stagna vadoso
perspicuus servat turbari nescia fundo
ac nitidum viridi lente trahit amne liquorem.
vix credas labi; ripis tam mitis opacis,   85
argutos inter volucrum certamine cantus,
somniferam ducit lucenti gurgite lympham.

18. A NIGHT SCENE
(Silius Italicus 7.282 – 307)

cuncta per et terras et lati stagna profundi
condiderat somnus, positoque labore dierum
pacem nocte datam mortalibus orbis agebat.
at non Sidonium curis flagrantia corda   285
ductorem vigilesque metus haurire sinebant
dona soporiferae noctis.   nam membra cubili
erigit et fulvi circumdat pelle leonis,
qua super instratos proiectus gramine campi
presserat ante toros.   tunc ad tentoria fratris   290
fert gressus vicina citos; nec degener ille
belligeri ritus, taurino membra iacebat
effultus tergo et mulcebat tristia somno.
haud procul hasta viri terrae defixa propinquae,
et dira e summa pendebat cuspide cassis;   295
at clipeus circa loricaque et ensis et arcus
et telum Baliare simul tellure quiescunt.
iuxta lecta manus, iuvenes in Marte probati;
et sonipes strato carpebat gramina dorso.
ut pepulere levem intrantis vestigia somnum: 300
'heus!' inquit pariterque manus ad tela ferebat,
'quae te cura vigil fessum, germane, fatigat?'
ac iam constiterat sociosque in caespite fusos
incussa revocat castrorum ad munera planta,
cum Libyae ductor: 'Fabius me noctibus aegris,   305
in curas Fabius nos excitat; illa senectus,
heu fatis quae sola meis currentibus obstat!'

15

19. FUNERAL PYRES AFTER CANNAE √
(Silius Italicus 10.527 – 542)

then, having
assigned
duties,
although
growing tired,
as quickly
as possible
they spread
the wood
here & there
among the
soldiers: a
tall leafy tree
ul two sides
was put fourth
continually.

                    tum munera iussa,
defessi quamquam, accelerant sparsoque propinquos
agmine prosternunt lucos: sonat acta bipenni
frondosis silva alta iugis. hinc ornus et altae   530
populus alba comae, validis accisa lacertis,
scinditur, hinc ilex, proavorum consita saeclo.
devolvunt quercus et amantem litora pinum
ac, ferale decus, maestas ad busta cupressos.
funereas tum deinde pyras certamine texunt,   535
officium infelix et munus inane peremptis,
donec anhelantes stagna in Tartessia Phoebus
mersit equos, fugiensque polo Titania caecam
orbita nigranti traxit caligine noctem.
post, ubi fulserunt primis Phaëthontia frena   540
ignibus, atque sui terris rediere colores,
supponunt flammam.

20. DESCRIPTION OF PAN √
(Silius Italicus 13.326 – 340)

Pan Iove missus erat, servari tecta volente
Troia, pendenti similis Pan semper et imo
vix ulla inscribens terrae vestigia cornu.
dextera lascivit caesa Tegeatide capra
verbera laeta movens festo per compita coetu.
cingit acuta comas et opacat tempora pinus,   330
ac parva erumpunt rubicunda cornua fronte;
stant aures, imoque cadit barba hispida mento.
pastorale deo baculum, pellisque sinistrum
velat grata latus tenerae de corpore dammae.
nulla in praeruptum tam prona et inhospita cautes,   335
in qua non, librans corpus similisque volanti,
cornipedem tulerit praecisa per avia plantam.
interdum inflexus medio nascentia tergo
respicit arridens hirtae ludibria caudae.   340

Pan, having
been sent by
love, wanting
to preserve
a Trojan
dwelling,
Pan, weighing
like
always
& going
hardly
inscribing
any
tracks
in the
earth
ul his
paws.

21. ROLL-CALL OF ROMAN HEROINES √
(Silius Italicus 13.806 – 822)

sed subito vultus monstrata Lavinia traxit.
nam virgo admonuit, tempus cognoscere manes
femineos, ne cunctantem lux alma vocaret.
'felix haec,' inquit, 'Veneris nurus ordine longo
Troiugenas iunxit sociata prole Latinis.   810

vis et Martigenae thalamos spectare Quirini?
Hersiliam cerne; hirsutos cum sperneret olim
gens vicina procos, pastori rapta marito
intravitque casae culmique e stramine fultum
pressit laeta torum et soceros revocavit ab armis.   815
aspice Carmentis gressus.   Evandria mater
haec fuit et vestros tetigit praesaga labores.
vis et, quos Tanaquil vultus gerat? haec quoque castae
augurio valuit mentis venturaque dixit
regna viro et dextros agnovit in alite divos.   820
ecce pudicitiae Latium decus, inclita leti
fert frontem atque oculos terrae Lucretia fixos.'

22. SCIPIO AND SYPHAX
(Silius Italicus 16.229 – 244)

iamque novum terris pariebat limine primo
egrediens Aurora diem, stabulisque subibant   230
ad iuga solis equi, necdum ipse ascenderat axem,
sed prorupturis rutilabant aequora flammis:
exigit e stratis corpus vultuque sereno
Scipio contendit Massyli ad limina regis.
illi mos patrius fetus nutrire leonum   235
et catulis rabiem atque iras expellere alendo.
tum quoque fulva manu mulcebat colla iubasque
et fera tractabat ludentum interritus ora.
Dardanium postquam ductorem accepit adesse,
induitur chlamydem, regnique insigne vetusti   240
gestat laeva decus; cinguntur tempora vitta
albente, ac lateri de more astringitur ensis.
hinc in tecta vocat, secretisque aedibus hospes
sceptrifero cum rege pari sub honore residunt.

STATIUS
Passages 23–32

23. AN AMBUSH
(Statius: Thebaid 2.496 – 526)

fert via per dumos propior, qua calle latenti
praecelerant densaeque legunt compendia silvae.
lecta dolis sedes: gemini procul urbe malignis
faucibus urgentur colles, quos umbra superni
montis et incurvis claudunt iuga frondea silvis—   500
insidias natura loco caecamque latendi
struxit opem—mediasque arte secat aspera rupes
semita, quam subter campi devexaque latis
arva iacent spatiis. contra importuna crepido,
Oedipodioniae domus alitis; hic fera quondam   505
pallentes erecta genas suffusaque tabo
lumina, concretis infando sanguine plumis
relliquias amplexa virum semesaque nudis
pectoribus stetit ossa premens visuque tremendo
conlustrat campos, si quis concurrere dictis   510
hospes inexplicitis aut comminus ire viator
audeat et dirae commercia iungere linguae;
nec mora, quin acuens exsertos protinus ungues
liventesque manus strictosque in vulnera dentes
terribili adplausu circum hospita surgeret ora;   515
et latuere doli, donec de rupe cruenta
heu! simili deprensa viro, cessantibus alis,
tristis inexpletam scopulis adfligeret alvum.
monstrat silva nefas: horrent vicina iuvenci
gramina, damnatis avidum pecus abstinet herbis;   520
non Dryadum placet umbra choris, non commoda sacris
Faunorum, diraeque etiam fugere volucres
prodigiale nemus. tacitis huc gressibus acti
deveniunt peritura cohors, hostemque superbum
adnixi iaculis et humi posita arma tenentes   525
exspectant densaque nemus statione coronant.

19

24. RUMOUR
(Statius: Thebaid 3.420 - 439)

et iam noctivagas inter deus armifer umbras   420
desuper Arcadiae fines Nemeaeaque rura
Taenariumque cacumen Apollineasque Therapnas
armorum tonitru ferit et trepidantia corda
implet amore sui.   comunt Furor Iraque cristas,
frena ministrat equis Pavor armiger.   at vigil omni   425
Fama sono vanos rerum succincta tumultus
antevolat currum flatuque impulsa gementum
alipedum trepidas denso cum murmure plumas
excutit: urget enim stimulis auriga cruentis
facta, infecta loqui, curruque infestus ab alto   430
terga comamque deae Scythica pater increpat hasta.
qualis ubi Aeolio dimissos carcere Ventos
dux prae se Neptunus agit magnoque volentes
incitat Aegaeo; tristis comitatus eunti
circum lora fremunt Nimbique Hiemesque profundae
Nubilaque et vulso terrarum sordida fundo   436
Tempestas: dubiae motis radicibus obstant
Cyclades, ipsa tua Mycono Gyaroque revelli,
Dele, times magnique fidem testaris alumni.

25. THE CHILD OPHELTES IN THE MEADOW
(Statius: Thebaid 4.786 - 796)

at puer in gremio vernae telluris et alto
gramine nunc faciles sternit procursibus herbas
in vultum nitens, caram modo lactis egeno
nutricem plangore ciens iterumque renidens
et teneris meditans verba inluctantia labris   790
miratur nemorum strepitus aut obvia carpit
aut patulo trahit ore diem nemorique malorum
inscius et vitae multum securus inerrat.
sic tener Odrysia Mavors nive, sic puer ales
vertice Maenalio, talis per litora reptans   795
improbus Ortygiae latus inclinabat Apollo.

26. A STORM AT SEA
(Statius: Thebaid 5.361 - 375)

iamque aberant terris, quantum Cortynia currunt
spicula, caeruleo gravidam cum Iuppiter imbri
ipsa super nubem ratis armamenta Pelasgae
sistit agens; inde horror aquis, et raptus ab omni
sole dies miscet tenebras, quis protinus unda   365

concolor; obnixi lacerant cava nubila venti
diripiuntque fretum, nigris redit umida tellus
verticibus, totumque notis certantibus aequor
pendet et arquato iamiam prope sidera dorso
frangitur, incertae nec iam prior impetus alno,   370
sed labat exstantem rostris modo gurgite in imo,
nunc caelo Tritona ferens.   nec robora prosunt
semideum heroum, puppemque insana flagellat
arbor et instabili procumbens pondere curvas
raptat aquas, remique cadunt in pectus inanes.   375

27. FUNERAL RITES
(Statius: Thebaid 6.54 - 73)

tristibus interea ramis teneraque cupresso
damnatus flammae torus et puerile feretrum   55
texitur: ima virent agresti stramina cultu;
proxima gramineis operosior area sertis,
et picturatus morituris floribus agger;
tertius adsurgens Arabum strue tollitur ordo
Eoas complexus opes incanaque glebis   60
tura et ab antiquo durantia cinnama Belo.
summa crepant auro, Tyrioque attollitur ostro
molle supercilium, teretes hoc undique gemmae
inradiant, medio Linus intertextus acantho
letiferique canes: opus admirabile semper   65
oderat atque oculos flectebat ab omine mater.
arma etiam et veterum exuvias cirumdat avorum
gloria mixta malis adflictaeque ambitus aulae,
ceu grande exsequiis onus atque immensa ferantur
membra rogo, sed cassa tamen sterilisque dolentes   70
fama iuvat, parvique augescunt funere manes.
inde ingens lacrimis honor et miseranda voluptas,
muneraque in cineres annis graviora feruntur.

28. INVOCATION OF THE MUSE
(Statius: Thebaid 8.373 - 394)

sed iam bella vocant: alias nova suggere vires,
Calliope, maiorque chelyn mihi tendat Apollo.
fatalem populis ultro poscentibus horam   375
admovet atra dies, Stygiisque emissa tenebris
Mors fruitur caelo bellatoremque volando
campum operit nigroque viros invitat hiatu,
nil vulgare legens, sed quae dignissima vita
funera, praecipuos annis animisque cruento   380

ungue notat; iamque in miseros pensum omne Sororum
scinditur, et Furiae rapuerunt licia Parcis.
stat medius campis etiamnum cuspide sicca
Bellipotens, iamque hos clipeum , iam vertit ad illos
arma ciens, aboletque domos, conubia, natos.   385
pellitur et patriae et, qui mente novissimus exit,
lucis amor; tenet in capulis hastisque paratas
ira manus animusque ultra thoracas anhelus
conatur, galeaeque tremunt horrore comarum.
quid mirum caluisse viros? flammantur in hostem   390
cornipedes niveoque rigant sola putria nimbo,
corpora ceu mixti dominis irasque sedentum
induerint: sic frena terunt, sic proelia poscunt
hinnitu tolluntque armos equitesque supinant.

29. A POET'S DEATH
(Statius: Thebaid 8.548 - 553)

sumpserat in Danaos Heliconius arma Corymbus,
ante comes Musis, Stygii cui conscia pensi
ipsa diu positis letum praedixerat astris   550
Uranie. cupit ille tamen pugnasque virosque,
forsitan ut caneret; longa iacet ipse canendus
laude, sed amissum mutae flevere sorores.

30. PARTHENOPAEUS' LAST WORDS
(Statius: Thebaid 9.885 - 907)

'labimur, i, miseram, Dorceu, solare parentem.   885
illa quidem, si vera ferunt praesagia curae,
aut somno iam triste nefas aut omine vidit.
tu tamen arte pia trepidam suspende diuque
decipito; neu tu subitus neve arma tenenti
veneris, et tandem, cum iam cogere fateri,   890
dic: merui, genetrix, poenas invita capesse;
arma puer rapui, nec te retinente quievi,
nec tibi sollicitae tandem inter bella peperci.
vive igitur potiusque animis irascere nostris,
et iam pone metus. frustra de colle Lycaei   895
anxia prospectas, si quis per nubila longe
aut sonus aut nostro sublatus ab agmine pulvis:
frigidus et nuda iaceo tellure, nec usquam
tu prope, quae voltus efflantiaque ora teneres.
hunc tamen, orba parens, crinem,' dextraque secandum
praebuit, 'hunc toto capies pro corpore crinem,   901
comere quem frustra me dedignante solebas.
huic dabis exequias, atque inter iusta memento,

[handwritten margin note:] Cornybus obtains force in the Greek Helicon, before the officials of poetry, In the Stygian, Uranie, whose knowledge pays off, by the position of the stars, she predicts his manner of dying for a short time.

ne quis inexpertis hebetet mea tela lacertis
dilectosque canes ullis agat amplius antris.   905
haec autem primis arma infelicia castris
ure, vel ingratae crimen suspende Dianae.'

31. SLEEP FALLS ON THE ARMY
(Statius: Thebaid 10.137 – 155)

ipse quoque et volucrem gressum et ventosa citavit
tempora, et obscuri sinuatam frigore caeli
implevit chlamydem, tacitoque per aethera cursu
fertur et Aoniis longe gravis imminet arvis.   140
illius aura solo volucres pecudesque ferasque
explicat, et penitus, quemcumque supervolat orbem,
languida de scopulis sidunt freta, pigrius haerent
nubila, demittunt extrema cacumina silvae,
pluraque laxato ceciderunt sidera caelo.   145
primus adesse deum subita caligine sensit
campus, et innumerae voces fremitusque virorum
submisere sonum; cum vero umentibus alis
incubuit piceaque haud umquam densior umbra
castra subit, errare oculi resolutaque colla,   150
et medio adfatu verba imperfacta relinqui.
mox et fulgentes clipeos et saeva remittunt
pila manu, lassique cadunt in pectora voltus.
et iam cuncta silent: ipsi iam stare recusant
cornipedes, ipsos subitus cinis abstulit ignes.   155

32. ACHILLES IN DISGUISE
(Statius: Achilleid 1.363 – 378)

accedit dictis pater ingenioque parentis
occultum Aeaciden—quis divum fraudibus obstet?—
accipit; ultro etiam veneratur supplice dextra   365
et grates electus agit: nec turba piarum
Scyriadum cessat nimio defigere visu
virginis ora novae, quantum cervice comisque
emineat quantumque umeros ac pectora fundat.
dehinc sociare choros castisque accedere sacris   370
hortantur, ceduntque loco et contingere gaudent.
qualiter Idaliae volucres, ubi mollia frangunt
nubila, iam longum caeloque domoque gregatae,
si iunxit pinnas diversoque hospita tractu
venit avis, cunctae primum mirantur et horrent: 375
mox propius propiusque volant, atque aere in ipso
paulatim fecere suam plausuque secundo
circumeunt hilares et ad alta cubilia ducunt.

COMMENTARY

1. LUCAN 1.33-66: INVOCATION TO NERO

The Greeks of the Hellenistic period had developed the notion
of a king as a god and contemporary Greek poets treated Augustus,
Tiberius, Gaius or Nero as gods equal in status to Zeus. This
idea was taken up by Virgil in *Georgics* 1.24-42 (Appendix pas-
sage a), to be followed by Horace in *Odes* 1.2. Both treat
Augustus as a deity on earth before he returns at death to
heaven to be an actual god. The concept of the emperor as a
god on earth was carried further by later poets and Lucan's
contribution here is significant both for its reworking of the
Georgics passage and for the sentiments he embodies in it. See
Williams (1978) 160ff.

In the preceding section (24-32) Lucan states the ruin and
depopulation of Italy; the blame belongs not to any foe but to
Italy herself. And yet (33-45) if that was the only way for
Fate to accomplish the accession of Nero, there can be no
complaint; all previous calamities were worth this one good
result. Lucan then turns to Nero himself, asking what god
will he be (46-52) and in what part of heaven will he reside
(53-59). The passage ends with a prayer for universal love
and peace (60-62) and with the assertion that for Lucan Nero
is already a god and sufficient inspiration to Roman poetry: there
is no need to invoke Greek deities like Apollo or Bacchus.

This passage is not intended as sarcastic - Williams (1978);
Jenkinson (1974); no grotesque exaggeration or distortion of
the Virgilian original can really be detected in it. It is
carefully balanced. In the first part 33-37 and 37-38 are
answered by 38-44 and 44-45 and the balance is maintained
between 46-52 (Nero's heavenly identity) and 53-59 (his abode
in heaven). The final seven lines, with their plea for
love and peace, give a surprising twist. It becomes
clear that, whereas peace generally meant to Virgil and Horace
freedom from civil war or at any rate peace imposed by Romans
and seen through Roman eyes, Lucan has the whole world in mind.
The words *inque vicem gens omnis amet* (61) probably reflect
Lucan's Stoicism, for the brotherhood of man was that school's
most important contribution to practical morality. The lines
appear to contradict the republicanism which is characteristic
of the epic as a whole - an inconsistency not unlike that which
Lucretius admits when he addresses Venus at the opening of *de
Rerum Natura* contrary to the Epicurean position which generally
saw traditional gods as utterly remote from human affairs.
Lucan was one of those to whom the bright hope of Nero's first
years of rule, with their cultural enlightenment, was an en-
couragement (see Introduction §9); Stoicism had no rooted
objection to monarchy provided that the monarch was virtuous.
It should be no surprise, therefore, to find Lucan enthusiastic
about the young Nero and the future of his reign. Indeed, the

first three books of the epic were published separately -
Dilke (1960) 5, n. 3 - and it is only thereafter that the tone
changes distinctly with the alteration in the relationship
between the poet and Nero.

34-37 magno: ablative of price; cf. Virgil, *Aeneid* 2.104 - *magno*
  mercentur Atridae.
parantur: simple for compound verb; *comparare* often = 'to buy',
  as in modern Italian *comprare* or Spanish *comprar.*
deis: dative of agent after passive verb.
gigantum: the Giants were sons of earth who tried to storm
  heaven. The gods repulsed them with the aid of Hercules and
  buried them under Aetna and other volcanoes.

38-44 These lines convey a concessive protasis, the apodosis
to which is in line 44: 'let Pharsalia fill her terrible plains
and let Carthaginian ghosts be glutted with blood, let the final
battle be joined at deadly Munda; to these disasters, Caesar,
let there be added the famine at Perusia and the horrors of
Mutina and the fleets that stormy Leucas keeps under her waves
and the slave wars near burning Aetna. In spite of all this
Rome owes a great debt to civil war because it was waged for
you'.
Pharsalia: the proper name of the battle, fought at Pharsalus in
  48 B.C.
saturentur: at the battle of Thapsus (46 B.C.) in modern Tunisia
  which was Hannibal's own country (around Carthage).
ultima ... proelia: plural for singular; the last battle of the
  Civil War was fought at Munda in Spain (45 B.C.), where Caesar
  defeated Labienus and Pompey's two sons.
Munda: ablative of place.
Caesar: i.e. Nero.
Perusina fames: the blockade in Perusia of the brother (Lucius
  Antonius) and wife (Fulvia) of Antony (Marcus Antonius) by
  Octavian during the winter of 41-40 B.C.
Mutinaeque labores: the fighting around Mutina and its siege in
  43 B.C. when Antony blockaded Decimus Brutus. In the event
  Antony was defeated.
fatis: 'disasters'.
classes: 'ships'.
Leucas: on the mainland of Acarnania in North-West Greece; but
  Actium is meant - by metonymy, in which the name of one thing
  is put for that of another related to it.
servilia bella: the war against Sextus Pompeius (who led an army
  largely composed of slaves) waged in Sicily by Agrippa on
  Octavian's behalf in 36 B.C.

45-47 acta ... peracta: Latin poetry did not reject, indeed it
  often played upon such jingles; cf. 2.160f. - *gestata ... con-
  gesta* or 3.348 - *contigi ... attingere.*
statione peracta: 'when your watch on earth is completed'.
serus: the hope is that the emperor will remain on earth as long
  as possible; for the flattery, cf. Ovid, *Metamorphoses*

15.868ff.; Silius Italicus 3.626f.; Statius, *Silvae* 1.1.105ff.
and 4.2.22.
praelati: 'preferred to earth', implying that death is a choice
within Nero's power.
polo: 'sky' - by synecdoche (part for the whole) from the original
astronomical meaning of *polus* ('pole'); and hence here 'the
dwellers in the sky', 'the gods'.

48-49 conscendere currus: Nero was a very keen charioteer
(Suetonius, *Nero* 53); he would be more fit to take the Sun-
god's place than Phaethon who lost his life trying to control
the solar chariot.
mutato sole: i.e. with Nero in place of Apollo as driver of the
solar chariot.

50-52 iuvet ... cedetur ... relinquet: for the change of mood,
cf. Horace, *Odes* 3.3.7f.- *si fractus inlabatur orbis, / impavidum
ferient ruinae*. The condition expressed by the subjunctive
iuvet is cancelled by the use of a vigorously prophetic future
indicative in *cedetur* and *relinquet*.
tibi numine ab omni / cedetur: 'every deity will give way to you'
- *cedetur* is impersonal passive.
iurisque tui: 'in your control', 'within your jurisdiction', a
prosaic expression.
quis deus esse velis ...: indirect question, a noun clause
governed by *relinquet*.

53-57 in Arctoo ... orbe: 'in the northern sky'; *Arctos*, the
Great and Lesser Bear constellations.
legeris: 'polite' future perfect.
nec polus ... Austri: 'nor where the sultry sky of the opposing
(*aversi* - lit. 'turned away') south sinks down (*vergitur*)'.
unde tuam ... Romam: 'whence you would look down with slanting
light on the Rome which is yours'. *sidus* can refer to the
sun, moon, a planet, a fixed star or a comet; here, by
metonymy, 'ray of light'.
aetheris ... si presseris unam, / sentiet axis onus: 'if you
put your weight upon one part of the infinite heavens, the
axis will feel the burden'. *axis*, 'the pole' (that is, either
end of the axis). Weight was regularly an attribute of
deities in antiquity.

57-59 librati: a proleptic use (whereby the employment of a word
anticipates its actual applicability) - 'keep the weight of
the universe (*caeli*) in balance (*librati*)'.
orbe ... medio: 'in the centre of the system', 'in the centre
of the whole'.
sereni: also used proleptically - 'fair, bright'.
vacet: 'may it be clear'.
a Caesare: lit. 'with Caesar as the point of departure' - cf.
such phrases as *a tergo, a fronte, a latere*; 'may no clouds
obstruct the view in Caesar's direction'.

60-62 sibi consulat: 'take thought for its own welfare'. For

the spirit of mutual love here, cf. 4.189ff., Lucan's appeal
to *Concordia*.
inque vicem: lit. 'in turn', but here = '*inter se*' (which
Lucan does not use).
missa: simple for compound verb - '*emissa*'.
Iani: the doors of Janus' temple were closed in time of peace.
Though referring to their closure with the arrival of peace
rather than their opening at the commencement of war, there
may here be a reminiscence of Ennius, *Annales* 266f. - *post-
quam discordia taetra / belli ferratos postes portasque refregit.*

63-66 numen: sc. *es*.
Cirrhaea: 'Delphic' by metonymy; Cirrha was the port of Delphi.
accipio ... velim: *velim* subjunctive apodosis - 'I would not
need to trouble the god who reveals his secrets at Cirrha' -
but the mood of the protasis remains indicative for emphasis
- 'if I admit you (as my inspiration)' implying 'and, of
course, I do'.
deum: Apollo, patron of poets.
Nysa: several places of this name claimed to be the birthplace
of Bacchus, for whom as god of poets see e.g. Horace, *Odes*
2.19.1; Ovid, *Amores* 3.1.23; 3.15.17; *Tristia* 5.3.33ff.;
Juvenal 7.64.

2.   LUCAN 1.524-549: PRODIGIES

Evidence of Lucan's profound interest in magic and the occult
appears thoughout his epic. The passage on prodigies from
which this excerpt derives is followed by a long description
(584-638) of entrail-examination (extispicy). Together they
are a remarkable indication of the poet's propensity for the
uncanny. (The excursus in book 5 in which Appius consults
the Delphic oracle (see passage 4 below), and the necromantic
séance in book 6 when Sextus Pompeius consults the Thessalian
witch Erichtho offer further examples of Lucan's pre-occupation
with the same kind of theme.)

After Caesar has summoned his forces from Gaul (1.392-465),
there is terror at Rome and the Senate flee (466-522). The
portents which accompanied these events are then described in
lines which should be compared with those of Virgil on the
prodigies at the time of Caesar's assassination (*Georgics*
1.463-492 - Appendix passage d below; cf. Ovid, *Metamorphoses*
15.779-802; Tibullus 2.5.71-78); comparison shows Lucan as
overheated and extravagant,

526-529 ignota ... sidera: 'stars hitherto unknown' - the meteors
and the comet to be described in the succeeding lines; cf.
passage 5 below, 560-564 n.
polum: here = 'sky' in general.
per inane: 'through the void of heaven' - recalling Lucretius
(1.1018, etc.).

faces: 'meteors'.

crinem: lit. 'the hair', but the reference is to the tail of a
comet.

et: 'that is to say'; *terris cometen* is not an addition to the
thought, but more precisely defines 'the hair of the baleful
star' (*crinemque timendi / sideris*).

mutantem regna: comets were believed to portend war, revolution,
the death of kings and rulers (cf. Statius, *Thebaid* 1.708 -
quae mutent sceptra cometae).

530-532 fallaci ... sereno: cf. Virgil, *Aeneid* 5.851 - *deceptus
fraude sereni*. Thunder in a clear sky frightened Horace
(*Odes* 1.34.5-8) into respecting the power of the gods.

et varias ...: 'and the flame (i.e. of the lightning) took
various shapes in the thick atmosphere (*denso ... aere*), at
one time its light being long like a javelin, at another
spread out like a torch (*lampas*)'.

533-539 tacitum: the clashing together of the clouds was thought
to be the cause of thunder and lightning (cf. Lucretius 6.99-
101; Ovid, *Metamorphoses* 8.339), and so lightning (especial-
ly without thunder) from a clear sky was certainly ominous.

Arctois: 'northern' (*Arctos, -i* feminine = 'the Great Bear');
cf. passage 1.53.

Latiare caput: i.e. Alba Longa (Castel Gandolfo), the ancient
head of the Latin league.

cornuque coacto: 'when her horns had been brought together' -
i.e. when her disc was completed at full moon.

redderet: 'reflected'.

terrarum: i.e. *orbis terrarum*.

540-544 Titan: 'the Sun'; *medio ... Olympo*: 'in the Zodiac'.

orbem: 'his own orb'.

qualem ...: 'even such a darkness (*noctem*) did Mycenae, the
city of Thyestes, draw upon itself when the sun fled back to
where he rose' - *per ortus*: *per* is substituted here for *in*
(see Introduction §28; no. 10). Thyestes was the brother of
Atreus, king of Mycenae, whose wife, Aerope, he seduced; he also
robbed Atreus of the golden-fleeced lamb given to him by
Hermes as a symbol of his right to rule. Atreus, for revenge,
killed the three sons of Thyestes and served them up to their
father at a banquet, which caused the Sun-god to flee in
revulsion and set in the east.

545-547 laxavit: 'opened'.

Mulciber: Vulcan.

vertice prono: 'eddying downwards'.

Hesperium ... latus: 'the coast of Italy'.

547-548 atra Charybdis: 'black Charybdis (a whirlpool) churned
up the sea from its depths (*fundo*) in bloody swirls'.

548-549 canes: the dogs are those of the sea-monster Scylla;
Virgil (*Aeneid* 3.428) describes them with dolphins' tails

joined to a womb full of wolves.

3. LUCAN 3.399-452: THE DRUIDS' GROVE

This incident (the felling of the Druids' grove) relates to
Caesar's siege of Massilia in 49 B.C.

Felling of trees had become a topos in Latin poetry. It starts
with Homer's description (*Iliad* 23.114-123) of gathering timber
for Patroclus' funeral pyre. Ennius took it up (*Annales* 187-
191), and it recurs in Virgil (*Aeneid* 6.179-185 - funeral rites
for Misenus; *Aeneid* 11.135-138 - burial of the dead during a
truce) and in Ovid (*Metamorphoses* 8.739-750 and 774-776 - the
impious Erysichthon's destruction of a grove). After Lucan
it is used by Silius Italicus (10.529ff. - fuel for funeral
pyres after Cannae - passage 19 below) and by Statius (*Thebaid*
6.84ff. - an expiatory rite; 12.50ff. - funeral rites of the
Thebans). Outside epic the younger Seneca (*Hercules Oetaeus*
1618ff. - a pyre for Hercules) had adopted the motif and Lucan
is particularly indebted to that passage. A comparison of the
passages cited with that in Virgil (Appendix passage e below)
shows that poet's strength and skill in handling the subject.
For detailed discussion, see Williams (1968) 263ff.

Groves were numinous places for the ancients, the haunt of
divinities or spirits (cf. Seneca, *Epistulae Morales*
41.3); to damage or destroy them was an act of impiety (cf. Ovid,
loc. cit. and 436 n. below). A Latin inscription as early as
the third century B.C. forbids the cutting down of trees in a
grove (Warmington (1957) 4.154); and it is worth comparing
Horace, *Epistles* 1.6.31-32 - *virtutem verba putas et / lucum
ligna*: ('if you think virtue is merely words and a grove
simply firewood'), a proverbial expression, here referring to
contemporary materialists who were prepared to cut down even
sacred groves.

Lucan clearly had an interest in the Druids. At 1.392-465
Lucan introduces a catalogue. In this he follows epic
practice going back to Homer's Catalogue of Ships in *Iliad*
2 or Virgil's list of Italian forces in *Aeneid* 7. But by a
bold and original stroke Lucan alters the traditional form of
lists of forces: he catalogues the dangerous tribes in Gaul
which were left unguarded when Caesar withdrew to invade
Italy. Within the catalogue he digresses on the religious
beliefs of the Druids (and he thus becomes a source for
Celtic religion).

400-401 cingens ...: 'enclosing with interlacing branches the
  dark air and cold shade, excluding the sunlight far above
  (*alte*)'.

402-405 Panes: cf. passage 20 below, and passage 23.522, n.
silvani: woodland spirits.

structae diris altaribus arae: 'the altars were piled with
hideous offerings'. *altaria*: here = 'that which is offered
on an altar' as opposed to its usual meaning, 'altar, high
altar'.
lustrata: 'sprinkled'.

406-411 siqua fidem ...: 'if antiquity, marvelling at the
gods, has deserved credit' - i.e. if any ancient marvel-
lous tale deserves belief. Cf. Virgil, *Aeneid* 10.792 - *si
qua fidem tanto est operi latura vetustas*.
lustris: 'lairs, dens'.
excussa: 'hurled'.
non ulli ...: 'and the trees while offering their foliage to
no breeze have a rustling (*horror*) of their own'.
411-413 nigris: the blackness of the water emphasises the
desolate nature of the place; it does not have a clear run-
ning stream flowing through it.

414-417 ipse situs ...: 'the very neglect and paleness of the
now rotting wood strikes men with dismay'.
non volgatis ... metuunt: 'men feel less awe of divinities
worshipped under common shapes (*volgatis ... figuris*)'.
tantum ... non nosse deos: 'so much does it add to their dread
not to know what gods they have to fear'. Cf. Virgil, *Aeneid*
8.349-352 - *iam tum religio pavidos terrebat agrestes / dira
loci, iam tum silvam saxumque tremebant. / hoc nemus, hunc,
inquit, frondoso vertice collem, / quis deus incertum est,
habitat deus*. Evander, conducting Aeneas to his home, tells
him the history of the place and points out features of the
scene which were to be famous in later times; here he is in-
dicating the most sacred grove where later the Capitol was to
stand.

417-421 et non ardentis ...: 'that the glare of burning came
from trees which were not on fire'.
circumfluxisse: 'twined round'.

422-423 cultu ... propiore: lit. 'with nearer worship' - i.e.
they kept their distance.
cessere deis: 'made way for the gods'.

423-425 medio cum Phoebus in axe est: 'when the sun is in mid-
heaven' - it was believed that the gods were especially angry
with those who disturbed their midday rest (cf. Theocritus
1.15-18; Homer, *Odyssey* 4.450ff.).
deprendere: 'to take unawares, surprise'.

426-428 inmisso: 'let loose upon'.

429-431 redituras: 'would rebound'.

432-437 torpore: 'lethargy'.
aeriam: cf. Virgil, *Eclogues* 1.59 - *nec gemere aeria cessabit
turtur ab ulmo*.

violata ... ferro: cf. Ovid, *Metamorphoses* 8.740f. and Hollis
(1970) ad loc. See, too, Appendix passage e below.

437-439 non sublato ...: 'not with their fear removed and
feeling safe (*secura*), having weighed against each other
the gods' and Caesar's anger' - i.e. and having decided
that Caesar was the more to be feared.

440-445 silvaque Dodones: i.e. the oak; Dodona in the mountains
of Epirus was the seat of an ancient oracle of Zeus whose will
was believed to be declared by the rustling of a sacred oak-
tree there.
alnus: see passage 5.596 n.
cupressus: cf. passage 19.534. *non plebeios*: 'royal' -
Cyparissus, son of King Telephus, was turned into a cypress.
propulsaque ...: 'and the wood when overthrown supported itself
by the close growth of the trees'.

445-449 laesos: cf. Virgil, *Aeneid* 1.8 - *quo numine laeso*.

450-452 utque satis ...: 'and when enough wood had been cut'.
curvoque soli ...: 'and the husbandmen wept for the year's
produce of the soil now resting from the curved plough, since
their oxen had been stolen from them'.
annum: the sense here of 'harvest' is occasionally found else-
where in poetry.

4.   LUCAN 5.169-197: FRENZY OF THE PROPHETESS

This excerpt forms part of the episode (5.71-236) in which
Appius Claudius consults the Delphic oracle. The comparison
between the Delphic prophetess and the Cumaean Sibyl (183)
shows Lucan consciously challenging Virgil's account of pro-
phetic frenzy (*Aeneid* 6.42-102). Virgil's treatment is care-
fully restrained; there is no long continuous description and
the episode falls into sections carefully balanced in tone and
intensity (Aeneas' prayer - 56-76; the height of the frenzy -
77-80; the prophecy - 81-87; the return to normal - 98-102;
see Appendix passage f below). The contrast between Virgil's
controlled style and language and Lucan's rhetoric is striking
(and it is worth comparing the latter with Seneca, *Agamemnon*
710ff. in the same vein).

Lucan's use of *Aeneid* 6 is divided. Here he directly challenges
a specific Virgilian description. But elsewhere the descent
into the underworld by Aeneas in search of his father's advice
is paralleled by Lucan (in *his* Book 6) by the summoning from
the underworld of the witch Erichtho for consultation by Sextus
Pompeius. Lucan there idiosyncratically reworks Virgil,
creating his own typically bizarre atmosphere.

The Silver epic poets found it hard to resist the appeal of
Aeneid 6. Silius' version (13.400-895) of the descent to the
underworld is very Virgilian. Scipio, after the death of
his father and uncle in Spain, happens to be resting near
Avernus, whence he makes the journey downwards. Silius
throws in elements from Homer as well; Scipio sees the Greek
poet amongst the shades in the midst of his epic heroes (13.
778ff.). Statius meets the challenge of *Aeneid* 6 in an
interesting way: in *Thebaid* 7.771-823 he describes the des-
cent of Amphiaraus to the underworld and the opening scene
of book 8 (1-126) is set there; later (*Thebaid* 10.156-218)
the weird prophetic ecstasy of Thiodamas is narrated. Statius
thus divides up his response to *Aeneid* 6 and in this sense may
be seen as Lucan's imitator and competitor.

169-174 aliena: i.e. not under her own control - 'frantic, she
careers about the cave, with her neck under possession'.
vittasque dei ... rotat: 'and having shaken off (*discussa* -
middle use of the participle - cf. passage 5.518 below n.
on *latus ... munita*) the fillets of the god and Phoebus'
garlands as her hair stood on end (*erectis ... comis*), with
tossing head (*ancipiti cervice*) she sends them whirling
(*rotat*) through the empty spaces of the temple'.
vaganti: dative after *obstantes* - '(tripods) which impede her
wandering course'.

174-177 'nor do you ply the lash alone and plunge the fiery
goad (*stimulos flammasque*) into her vitals (*viscera*); she
has to bear the curb as well' - cf. Virgil, *Aeneid* 6.100-101 -
*ea frena furenti / concutit et stimulos sub pectore vertit
Apollo* (Appendix passage f below).
nec tantum ...: 'nor is the priestess allowed to reveal all she
is allowed to know'.

177-182 venit aetas ... congeriem: 'all future time gathers into
one mass'.
nititur in lucem: 'struggles to the light'.
vocemque petentia fata / luctantur: 'destinies compete in seeking
utterance'.
non ... derat: denial of the opposite of what is meant (litotes)
- 'there were present to her ...'.
modus Oceani: 'the compass of the Ocean'.

183-189 vates Cumana: 'the Sibyl (prophetess) of Cumae' -
Cumae in Campania was founded by settlers from Chalcis in
Euboea (*Euboico*); cf. Virgil, *Aeneid* 6.2 - *et tandem Euboicis
Cumarum adlabitur oris*.
recessu: 'cave'.
indignata ...: 'resenting that her frenzy should be at the
service of many nations'.
ex tanta ...: 'out of so great a heap of destinies she picked
out those of Rome with a haughty hand'. Lucan's comparison
of one prophetess with another is hardly effective; it adds

... .hing to the sense and simply serves to draw attention to
his Virgilian source.
Phemonoe: the name of the Delphic prophetess.
te: i.e. 'your fate' - Appius is being addressed (Appi 188).
   For the use of apostrophe, compare 174 above and Introduction
   §39.
consultor operti / Castalia tellure dei: 'you who came to consult
   the god hidden in the Castalian (i.e. Delphic) land'.
vix: 'with difficulty'.
inter fata ...: 'long searching for you concealed amongst so
   many fates'.

190-197 tum: when she had located the fate of Appius. The
   exaggerated quality of Lucan's description here is partic-
   ularly noteworthy.
anhelo clara: 'murmurs uttered loudly (clara) with panting
   breath (meatu refers to respiration)'.
extremae: 'finally, at last'.
domita iam virgine: 'when the maiden was mastered'; cf. Aeneid
   6.79-80 - tanto magis ille (i.e. Pheobus) fatigat / os rabidum,
   fera corda domans, fingitque premendo.
effugis: prophetic present - she sees the future taking place
   before her eyes.
quietem: Appius died in Euboea and was buried there. He was
   not to die in battle (solus), but by a natural death.

5. LUCAN 5.504-596: AMYCLAS

The most popular of Lucan's figures in the Middle Ages was
Amyclas, the poor fisherman whom Caesar asks to ferry him
from Palaestra to Italy. Dante gives a spirited translation
of the passage (Convivio 4.13.12), and uses it also in the
Paradiso (11.67ff.) where Poverty, the bride of St. Francis
of Assisi, dwells unalarmed in the house of the humble Amyclas.
(For the mediaeval use of the Amyclas motif, see E. R. Curtius,
European Literature and the Latin Middle Ages, trans. W. R.
Trask (London, 1953) 187 and 200.)

Praise of poverty or denunciation of wealth became a topos in
ancient literature; Lucan's Caesar-Amyclas scene is reminiscent
of the literary tradition concerning the reception of a god or
hero into a simple home. It first appears in Eumaeus' hospi-
tality to Odysseus (Homer, Odyssey 14), and became popular in
Hellenistic poetry: Callimachus in the Aetia described the
entertainment of Hercules by a poor man called Molorchus and
that of Theseus by a poor old woman in his Hecale. Ovid's
story of Baucis and Philemon's reception in their humble
dwelling of Jupiter and Mercury (Metamorphoses 8.631ff.) shows
Callimachean influence and was probably used in turn by the
poet of the Moretum. In Paradise Lost 5.308ff. Adam and Eve
entertain the archangel Raphael and Ovid was Milton's model.

Relevant, too, to this theme is Aeneid 8.280-369 in which king

Evander, exiled with his followers from Arcadia and settled
in Italy, tells Aeneas of the early history of Latium and the
Golden Age under Saturnus, and conducts him on a tour of his
little city, pointing out places destined to be famous in
Roman history. Virgil certainly commends to his Augustan
contemporaries (as also does Tibullus) simple sufficiency as
an objective in life and there may even be a hint about the
frugal life-style of Augustus himself (cf. Suetonius, *Augustus*
72; R. Heinze, *Hermes* 65 (1930) 385ff.). Evander's words of
invitation to Aeneas (*Aeneid* 8.364-365:

> *aude, hospes, contemnere opes et te quoque dignum*
> *finge deo, rebusque veni non asper egenis*)

became proverbial. Seneca twice quotes them (*Epistulae Morales*
18.12 and 31.11) for his own Stoic purpose, and Juvenal alludes
to them in apologising for a simple meal (11.60-63).

The image of the hero who 'stoops' humbly to enter a small
house is interestingly studied by Gransden (1976) 26-29, who
traces it from the *Odyssey* (Eumaeus and Odysseus) through
classical writers to Spenser, Shakespeare and Marvell, re-
marking that it was regarded in the Renaissance as an allegorical
prefiguration of Christian teaching.

The storm at sea which is an important feature of the Amyclas
story had also become a topos. The tradition begins with
Homer, *Odyssey* 5.291ff. and there were storm-scenes in Livius
Andronicus' *Odyssia*, a Latin version of the Greek poem in the
native Italic Saturnian metre, and in his tragedy *Aegisthus*.
The first book of Naevius' *Bellum Punicum* also contained a
storm and the tragedian Accius helped to fix the details,
especially in his *Clytemnestra*. From Ennius' *Annales* a fine
storm simile survives (430-432), but the most famous of early
Latin storms is that from Pacuvius' *Teucer* (350-365; Warmington
(1957); Williams (1968) 646). Virgil's storm at the beginning
of the *Aeneid* (1.81-123; Austin (1971) *ad loc.*; Appendix pas-
sage g below) looks back to the archetype in the *Odyssey* with
some influence from Naevius. Virgil's sense of proportion in
handling the subject can be appreciated through comparison with
later descriptions: Ovid, *Metamorphoses* 11.474ff.; Lucan 4.48ff.
(the Spanish floods), 9.319ff. (the storm off the Syrtes) and
9.445ff. (the Libyan dust storm); Seneca, *Agamemnon* 462ff.;
Valerius Flaccus 1.608ff. - passage 8 below; Statius, *Thebaid*
5.361-375 - passage 26 below; Quintus Smyrnaeus 14.488ff. The
locus had also spread into prose (e.g. Livy 21.58 and 40.58;
Tacitus, *Annales* 2.23) and it became part of the exercises in
the schools of rhetoric (elder Seneca, *Controversiae* 7.1.4
and 10; cf. the parody by Petronius, *Satyricon* 114). (The
classic modern description of a storm at sea is Conrad's 'The
Nigger of the *Narcissus*' (1897) ch.3.) For the whole subject,
see Rutz (1970) 171ff.; Friedrich (1956); Morford (1967) ch.3
- 'The Literary Background to Lucan's Storms' - and ch.4 -

'Lucan's Storms: Analysis and Discussion'; Barratt (1979) 144ff.

504-509 fessas nox languida curas: chiastic word-order. *nox languida:* cf. *Aeneid* 12.908-909 - *ac velut in somnis, oculos ubi languida pressit / nocte quies.*

fortuna minor: 'their lower station, rank'. Office has its cares, the lowly sleep more soundly. The sentiment and the picture of the restless general among his sleeping troops may be worth comparison with Shakespeare's treatment of the eve of Agincourt in *Henry V* (cf. passage 18 below).

iam ... iam: anaphora (repetition of the same word at the beginning of successive clauses).

tertia ... vigiles ... hora secundos: symmetrical interweaving of cases, with the adjectives enclosing the nouns. *tertia:* the first watch ended at the third hour of the night.

famulis: 'slaves'; *famulus* and *famula, minister* and *ministra* are generally preferred in Latin poetry to *servus*, though Virgil has *serva* (*Aeneid* 5.284 and 9.546).

510-514 egressus: transitively used, as also *transsiluit* with *membra* as object.

quod fallere posset: 'because he was able to escape notice (through their lack of vigilance)'. Cf. Virgil, *Aeneid* 9.314-315 - *egressi superant fossas noctisque per umbram / castra inimica petunt* - where Nisus and Euryalus begin their night attack; like them, Caesar moves by night but his is not an honourable enterprise, arising as it does from personal ambition.

515-518 sterili iunco cannaque intexta palustri: cf. Ovid, *Metamorphoses* 8.630 - *parva (domus) quidem stipulis et canna tecta palustri* (of the simple home of Baucis and Philemon). Lucan's line is clearly derivative of Ovid (did Ovid perhaps write *texta*?).

latus ... munita: accusative of respect with a passive participle - originally a Greek construction, though the accusative of the direct object with a middle participle seems to have been a native Latin use.

inversa ... phaselo: 'with an upturned skiff' - Gk. *phaselos,* lit. 'a bean-pod', hence the name for a vessel of similar shape.

519ff. Note the simple life led by Amyclas, contrasting with the self-seeking of Caesar; cf. Virgil, *Aeneid* 8.280-369 (see introduction to this passage above).

521-523 quisnam: the suffix *-nam* attached to interrogative pronouns or adverbs adds strength and urgency to the question while rendering the interrogative term itself somewhat vague and indeterminate.

523-527 aggere iam tepidae sublato fune favillae: 'having lifted the rope from the pile (*aggere*) of cool ashes (*tepidae*

*favillae)' - the rope would be kept thus smouldering to
prevent the fire from being extinguished completely.
pavit: lit. 'nourished' (from *pascere*); cf. Virgil, *Georgics*
2.432 - *pascunturque ignes*; *Aeneid* 2.684 - *lambere flamma
comas et circum tempora pasci*. In prose *alere* occurs of a
flame in the same sense.
securus belli: genitive of respect - a poetic usage; cf.
Lucan 1.212 - *tanti securus volneris*; 4.534 - *securaque
pugnae*, etc.
praedam ... scit non esse casas: 'he knows that the dwellings
of the poor provide no booty for those engaged in civil
war'.

527-531 o vitae tuta facultas ...: apostrophe extolling
simplicity of lifestyle (cf. Lucan, 1.160ff.; 4.373ff.;
9.424ff.) - 'how safe and easy are the poor man's life and
his humble home (*lares*)'. The praise of poverty is particu-
larly Stoic. (On apostrophe with moralising, see Introduction
§§39-41.)
o munera nondum / intellecta deum: 'how blind are people still
to the gifts of the gods' - poverty is a divine gift en-
suring safety.
quibus ... contingere templis ... muris ... trepidare ...?: 'What
temples or walled cities (*muris*) could claim as much as this,
that they feel no shock of alarm (*nullo trepidare tumultu*)
when Caesar's hand knocks?'; *contingere* (lit. 'to happen,
come to pass, turn out') with dative and infinitive is
poetic and in prose is post-Augustan.

531-535 spesque tuas laxa: 'enlarge your hopes'.
Hesperiam: local accusative ('place to which').
si ... vehis ... debebis: the combination of present and future
in conditional sentences occurs from time to time also in
prose.
importunamve fereris / pauperiem deflens: added by Housman to
assist the sense - 'if you obey my orders and carry me to
Italy, you will not henceforth (*ultra*) owe everything to
your boat and your own hands, nor will you be said (*fereris*)
to have spent (*duxisse*) a needy old age bewailing your cruel
poverty', i.e. Caesar will richly reward him. However,
Housman's supplement is hardly necessary; the Latin still
yields good sense without it - '... you will not henceforth
owe everything to your boat, and to the labour of your hands
the dragging out (*duxisse* - verbal noun, object after *debebis*)
of a needy old age'.

536-537 ne cessa: archaic imperative form, probably intended as
part of Caesar's lofty style of speech; cf. 539 below.

538-539 indocilis privata loqui: 'unable to speak like a
private (i.e. ordinary) man'. There is a ceremonious elabor-
ation in Caesar's form of address.
indocilis: 'unteachable' (cf. *indoctus*, 'untaught').

539ff. Amyclas foretells the storm. A similar piece of didact-
icism in Lucan is at 8.167-184, where the helmsman instructs
Pompey in the meaning of the stars. Here lines 541-545 deal
with the sun; 546-550 with the moon; and 551-556 with ter-
restrial signs presaging winds.

541-543 concordesque ... radios: 'symmetrical rays', as opposed
   to *diducta luce* (543 - 'with divided beams'). *concordesque*
   = *neque concordes* - the *-que* here carries on the negative.
Noton altera Phoebi / altera pars Borean diducta luce vocabat:
   'with divided beams one half of the Sun (*Phoebi*) summoned the
   south wind (*Noton*, Greek accusative), the other half the
   north wind'.

544-545 orbe quoque ...: 'also, the centre of his orb was
   hollowed (*exhaustus* equivalent to *exesa* (547 below) of the
   moon) and he set weak (i.e. dim), having allowed, his light
   being feeble, eyes to gaze upon him'.

546ff. The ultimate source for the moon as a weather sign is
the Hellenistic Greek *Phaenomena* of Aratus which had been
translated into Latin by Cicero. Virgil makes extensive use
of *Phaenomena* in *Georgics* 1; both he (*Georgics* 1.427-433,
Appendix passage h below) and Lucan take from Aratus three
points about the moon as a weather sign: dullness forecasts
rain, redness wind, and brightness fair weather. The weather
signs based on behaviour of birds are also drawn from Aratus by
way of Virgil (see 551-556 n. below).

546-550 lunaque non ...: 'and the moon when she rose (*surrexit*)
   did not shine (*lucida*) with slender horn, nor was she carved out
   (*exesa*) in clear-cut (*puros*) hollows (*recessus*) of her central
   orb'. *-que non*: also found in prose.
non ... aut: *aut* carries on the negative (cf. 552-553, *nec ...
   aut*).
exesa: Greek accusative of respect with a passive participle -
   see 518 n. on *latus ... munita* above. *puros ... recessus*:
   poetic plural.
nec duxit ...: 'nor did she prolong her tapering extremities
   (*tenuata cacumina*) with upright horn'.
notam rubuit: *rubuit* is transitive (lit. 'she reddened her indi-
   cation of storms', i.e. 'growing red, she gave warning of
   storms'). This transitive usage is apparently an innovation
   on Lucan's part.
tum lurida pallens / ora tulit voltu sub nubem tristis ituro:
   'then being pale she showed a sallow face (*lurida ... ora*),
   being sad as her countenance began to disappear behind a cloud'.

551-556 litoris ictus: 'the waves beating on the shore'.
incertus qui ...: 'the dolphin which in wavering course
   (*incertus*) challenges the sea (to rise)'.
siccum: 'the dry land'.
mergus: 'gull', or perhaps 'cormorant'.

ardea: 'heron'; cf. Virgil, *Georgics* 1.363f. - *notasque*
  paludes / deserit atque altam supra volat ardea nubem.
sublimis: used adverbially.
pinnae: i.e. *alae* (by synecdoche).
natanti: here 'cleaving the water'.
quodque caput ... litora cornix: cf. Virgil, *Georgics* 1.388ff. -
  tum cornix plena pluviam vocat improba voce / et sola in sicca
  secum spatiatur harena. *velut*: *velut si* would be more usual
  in prose. *occupet*: the meaning 'forestall' for *occupare* is
  poetic.
instabili gressu: 'with lurching gait' - different from Virgil's
  spatiatur with its implication of stateliness; on Virgil's
  selective and creative use of Aratus on weather signs, see
  Williams (1968) 258ff. *metitur*: 'paces, traverses' (a poetic
  use).

557-559 magnarum ... discrimina rerum: 'a great crisis'.
praebere manus: 'give assistance' (cf. 'lend a hand').

560ff. The storm rises. Its literary basis is to be found in
a number of Virgilian storms: *Aeneid* 1.81ff. (Aeneas is de-
flected from Italy by Aeolus at the behest of Juno, see Ap-
pendix passage g); 2.416ff. (a brief simile); 3.192ff. (the Trojans
endure a storm at sea for three days and nights - cf. 5.8ff.,
where some of the same details are repeated).

560-564 ad quorum motus ...: 'at the motion of the winds, not
  only did meteors (*sidera*) gliding through the high heaven
  draw in their wake trains of dispersed light (*sulcos* = lit.
  'furrows') as they fell (*cadentia*), but also the stars which
  remain fixed in the summit of the sky seemed to be shaken'.
  Shooting stars and comets portended war (cf. Lucan 1.527ff.,
  passage 2 above; and perhaps Virgil, *Aeneid* 5.519ff.). The 's'
  alliteration in these lines, the chiasmus *summis ... fixa ...*
  astra polis, and the hyperbole (even the fixed stars are
  moved by the winds) should be noted.

564-567 niger inficit horror / terga maris: cf. Virgil, *Aeneid*
  3.195 - *inhorruit unda tenebris.* *horror* is both 'a bristling,
  trembling, shuddering, dread' and 'awe, thrill'. *niger*:
  used by Lucan 14 times, *ater* 16 times; *ater* is a specifically
  epic word and predominates in Virgil and Silius (and Senecan
  tragedy). Of *ater* Valerius Flaccus has 15 instances, Statius
  45; and of *niger* Valerius 14, Statius 49.
volumina: from *volvere* = 'to roll'; 'the threatening sea (*unda*
  minax) boiled (*aestuat*) over a vast expanse (*longo ... tractu*)
  as wave rolled after wave'.
flatusque incerta ...: 'the stormy sea, uncertain of the coming
  gale, gave witness that it was pregnant with tempest';
  turgida (for *turbida*) was suggested by Housman as being more
  consonant with the metaphor in *conceptos*.

568ff. This speech may be compared with that of Palinurus in
similar circumstances (Virgil, *Aeneid* 5.13-25, Appendix passage

i below).

568-570 trepidae: transferred epithet; it is the *rector* him-
self who is *trepidus*.
Zephyros ... Austros: poetic plurals.

571-576 consulimus: present with future meaning.
Cori veniet mare: 'the sea will come under the sway of the
north-west wind' (cf. Valerius Flaccus 2.506 - *nubiferi
venit unda Noti*).
longe nimium: *longe* for *longinqua*; 'or else the nearest land
may prove too distant'.

577ff. The confident tone of Caesar's speech contrasts with
the hesitation of Amyclas. The difference, too, between Lucan's
Caesar and Virgil's Aeneas is remarkable - compare 579-580 with
Aeneid 5.17-18; 588-589 with *Aeneid* 5.28; and 592-593 (Fortune
as subservient to Caesar's aims) with *Aeneid* 5.22, where
Palinurus acknowledges her power.

579-583 caelo auctore: 'when heaven is guarantor'.
vectorem: *vector* is both 'a bearer, carrier' and 'a passenger'
- here in the latter sense, though Lucan (6.392) also has
it in the former. *de quo male tunc fortuna meretur, / cum post
vota venit*: 'whom Fortune treats badly when she merely comes
in answer to his prayers'.

584-586 Caesare: ablative of instrument - found in classical
prose, commonly with *stipatus* and *comitatus*, but otherwise
it is employed of people who could be considered to be
instruments rather than agents (e.g. soldiers, slaves). It
is more often found in poetry (where it was useful for
metrical reasons) and in later writers.
onus: 'the cargo, freight' (i.e Caesar himself).

586-588 mora: here 'duration, continuation'.
proderit undis / ista ratis: 'that boat of yours will benefit
the sea' - because on account of Caesar the winds which are
stirring it up will be calmed. Caesar, as presented by
Lucan, has no small view of his own importance and influence.

588-591 fuge proxima velis / litora: *velis* perhaps instrumental
ablative ('make use of your sails to escape the neighbouring
shore') or else dative ('flee from the shore nearest to your
sails').

591-593 quaerit ...: 'Fortune seeks a boon she may confer on
me'.

593-596 mālum: from *mālus* ('mast').
alnus: (feminine) 'alder' and hence by metonymy 'ship, boat'.

6.   LUCAN 8.698-711: POMPEY'S NEGLECTED CORPSE

Pompey has been assassinated when seeking refuge in Egypt
(8.560-636). His widow Cornelia has lamented his loss (637-
662), and his head has been cut off and embalmed, an event
described in gruesome detail (663-691). This excerpt con-
tains reflection on his death. Moralising (see Introduction
§§40-41) has a long history in classical literature; Roman
writers were always prone to it. Often the influence of
Stoicism can be perceived and Lucan follows the lead of his
Stoic uncle, the younger Seneca, in his moralising (see
Introduction §8).

Lucan certainly had Virgil's picture of the butchery of Priam
at the hands of Pyrrhus (*Aeneid* 2.506-558) in mind when he
wrote these lines. The coda of Virgil's description (2.554-
558, Appendix passage j below) marks the climax of the sack
of Troy as Virgil conceived it - a brief, restrained piece
of moralising on the end of an epoch, allowing some relief
after the high tension of the narrative (Austin (1964) *ad
loc.*). Lucan's tactic is by sheer contrast *grand Guignol*:
he characteristically devotes a whole grisly passage (667ff.)
to the decapitation of Pompey's corpse and cannot resist
returning to the subject as he moralises on Pompey's fate.
In Virgil the decapitation of Priam receives only brief mention
(558 - *avulsumque ... caput*) at the epilogue.

698-700 feriunt: bold use of what Postgate calls 'inverted
   passive'; it is the body that strikes the shore, not *vice
   versa*.
truncus: adjective.

701-707 hac ... fide: grim irony; *fides* includes the ideas of
   'consistency' and 'punctiliousness'. Fortune kept herself
   and her favourite to their agreement; the repetition (anaphora)
   of the pronoun *hac* underlines her persistence.
pertulit: 'carried to the end'.
morte petit: seemingly 'aimed at him with a deadly shaft'; for
   mors as 'the means whereby death is effected' cf. 6.486 - *et
   mortibus instruit artes*. *petit*: perfect (*petiit* contracted).
   morte: for the ablative cf. Virgil, *Georgics* 2.505 - *petit
   excidiis urbem miserosque penates*.
exegit: 'demanded of him' (as payment in return for his past
   prosperity).
quibus inmunes: *inmunis*, 'free from service, obligation ...
   unaffected by ...'.
nullo ...: the ablatives qualify the adjectives; 'happy with no
   god to trouble him, wretched with none to spare him'.

707-708 inpulit: 'overthrew'.
dilata ... manu: 'with stroke delayed, deferred'.

708-711 pulsatur harenis: cf. 698 above - *feriunt*.

hausto: drawn through his wounds.
ludibrium pelagi: an echo of 7.380, *ludibrium soceri* - a fate
  which Pompey had there prayed to avoid.
una nota est Magno ...: the one mark of distinction left to
  Magnus is the absence of the severed head. *Magno* is strongly
  ironical.

7. LUCAN 9.1-18: POMPEY DEAD

Pompey's soul here ascends from the funeral pyre to the
heavens. Lucan bases his description on the ascension of
Scipio in Cicero's *Somnium Scipionis*, which follows a
Platonising Stoicism made popular in Rome by Posidonius of
Apamea (ca. 135 - ca. 55 B.C.). Scipio has a dream in which
he is shown the heavenly habitation of great and righteous
spirits and is told to prepare himself for such a dwelling
after death. In Lucan Pompey arrives (9.5) *qua niger astri-*
feris conectitur axibus aer ('where the murky air joins the
star-bearing wheels'); i.e. he reaches the frontier between
air and aether ('upper atmosphere'), between Aristotle's
'Nature' and 'Sky'. This is evidently at the orbit of the moon
since the region of the air is 'what lies between the countries
of earth and the lunar movements' (6 - *quodque patet terras*
inter lunaeque meatus). The region is inhabited by *semidei*
manes (7), the ghosts of good men who are now demigods. They
seem to inhabit the very surface of air, almost in the aether
itself (8 - *patientes aetheris imi* ('able to bear - perhaps
breathe - the lowest aether')), as if the aether grew more like
air or the air more like aether at their meeting-point. Here
Pompey first fills himself with 'true light' (11-12 - *se lumine*
vero / inplevit) and sees (13) 'under how vast a night lies what
we call day' (but cf. 13 n. below). Finally (14) *risitque sui*
ludibria trunci - he looks down and sees the mockeries done to
his corpse, which was having a scarcely dignified funeral, and
he laughs.

The Stoic philosophy in this passage and its source in the
Somnium are clear, but a literary motif also contributed to its
creation. Homer (*Odyssey* 5.44-54) has Hermes fly to Ogygie
with orders for Calypso to send Odysseus away; this is taken up
by Virgil whose Mercury flies to convey a message to Aeneas,
reminding him of his destiny and ordering him to sail from
Carthage (*Aeneid* 4.238-261). Virgil vividly describes Mercury's
journey, imagining him looking down on Mount Atlas and thus
creatively reworking the Homeric motif by his addition of the
aerial view of the earth below. Such a bird's-eye view is
treated in greater detail by Ovid (*Metamorphoses* 2.702-731),
representing Mercury on a similar journey. Statius uses the
idea twice: *Thebaid* 1.92-124 (Tisiphone on her way to Thebes
in answer to Oedipus' prayer); and *Thebaid* 2.55-92 (the ghost
of Laius flying by night to Thebes), a very striking passage,
perhaps based on Lucan here but with the impression powerfully
conveyed of what it is like to view a dark world from a great

height. (The long description of Julius Caesar's apotheosis by Ovid (*Metamorphoses* 15.746ff.) would have been known to Lucan but no connection between the two passages seems traceable.)

1-4 at non in Pharia ...: 'but Pompey's spirit (*manes*) did not linger (lit. 'lie') in the Egyptian ashes'. *Pharius*: 'belonging to Pharos', an island in the Bay of Alexandria, where king Ptolemy Philadelphus built a famous light-house (hence French, *le phare*), and so 'Egyptian'.
sequitur: 'makes for'.
convexa Tonantis: 'the dome of the Thunderer'. *convexus* as an adjective, 'vaulted, arched; sloping, steep'; whence the neuter noun *convexum*, 'vault, arch' and so as here, 'the vault of heaven' (cf. *Aeneid* 4.451 - *taedet caeli convexa tueri*).

5-11 quodque patet ...: see introduction to this passage above for translation and interpretation of this section.
ignea virtus: 'fiery quality'. For the Stoics the soul was a mixture of air and fire held together in tension.
innocuos vita: 'guiltless in their lives'.
non illuc ...: Lucan seems to assume that the higher reaches of virtue are inaccessible to the rich and that therefore their spirits after death cannot attain the celestial abode he is describing.

11-14 astra / fixa polis: 'the fixed stars of heaven'; *polus* is the 'pole of the earth; the sky, the heavens'; the plural is poetic.
vidit quanta sub nocte iaceret / nostra dies: the meaning could either be 'he saw how dark, compared with the aether, our terrestrial day is', or 'he saw under how huge an abyss of nocturnal phenomena (i.e. stars, cf. 11, 12, 13) our terrestrial day takes place'. The former is more probable; the ascending spirit passes into a region compared with which our terrestrial day is only a sort of night.
ludibria trunci: 'the mockery done to his headless corpse' (cf. passage 6.710 n. above).

15-18 Emathiae: Emathia was the part of Macedonia nearest to Thessaly (where Pharsalus was).
Bruti ... Catonis: appropriately Pompey's spirit descends upon Brutus and Cato who are the principal symbols of the republican cause; Brutus was to be one of Caesar's assassins, and Cato was to continue the fight in Africa.

8. VALERIUS FLACCUS 1.608-642: STORM AT SEA

Valerius' primary model was the *Argonautica* of Apollonius
of Rhodes. The Roman poet is often superior to his Greek
predecessor in the matter of probability. His heroes, for
example, do not, as in Apollonius, take to the sea as though
they had been used to it all their lives; the ancients had
a dread and distrust of the sea and Valerius' Argonauts are
the first sailors in history, risking their lives on an ele-
ment entirely new to them - a point emphasised in this and the
following passage (9).

Apollonius had not, in fact, included a storm but by the time
of Valerius such descriptions had become a literary topos (see
introduction to passage 5 above). Valerius' version should be
compared with those of Lucan (passage 5 above) and Statius
(passage 26 below). On each of these passages the influence
of Virgil (*Aeneid* 1.81-123 - Appendix passage g below) is strong.
Where Virgil is compact and varied, Valerius, like all the
Silver epic poets, is more diffuse. For instance he begins
(610ff.) with all four principal winds, giving each elaborate
description. In comparison, Virgil mentions only three with-
out elaboration; the upsurge of his storm is economically and
effectively covered (81-91); Aeneas' despairing speech provides
variety, a break from intense description, that Valerius fails
to achieve in the Argonauts' 'cry' (624-632) which merely con-
tains further description of the storm and more intensity;
treatment of the storm's effects (102-113) rounds off Virgil's
presentation giving it a balance and control which Valerius
cannot match.

608-609 **fremere**: historic infinitive (also *poscere*).
intus: i.e. within the cave of Aeolus where the winds are kept
  imprisoned.
aequora ... poscere: 'began to clamour for the open sea'.

609-610 contorto turbine: *contortus*, 'intricate, confused, com-
  plicated; vigorous, vehement'; 'struck (*impulit*) with a
  powerful blast the mighty door'.
Hippotades: Aeolus (son of Hippotes).

610-617 fundunt se carcere ...: 'there burst joyfully forth
  from their prison the Thracian horses (of the north wind),
  the West wind and the south wind of the night-dark wings in
  company with the progeny of the storm-clouds, and the east
  wind, his hair wild (*hispidus*) with the blasts and yellow
  with much sand'. *concolor* goes with *nocti* ('having the same
  colour as night'); *alas* and *crinem* are both accusatives of
  respect, the former after *concolor*, the latter after *hispidus*.
flavus: cf. Virgil, *Aeneid* 7.31 - *multa flavus harena* (Tiber-
  inus the river-god).
piceoque ... caelo: '(and night buries all) beneath a pitchy
  sky'.

618-621 **excussi manibus remi**: cf. Virgil, *Aeneid* 9.474 - *excusso manibus radii*. **conversaque frontem / puppis**: lit. 'the ship was turned in respect of its head', i.e. 'was driven off course'.
in obliquum resonos latus accipit ictus: 'receives on to its side turned aslant the resounding shocks'. Cf. Virgil, *Aeneid* 1.104ff.; Lucretius 3.628 - *per obliquum crebros latus accipit ictus*.
malum: *mālus, -i* (masculine), 'upright pole, mast, prop'; cf. Lucan 5.595-596 (passage 5 above) - *fragilemque super volitantia malum / vela tulit*.

621-624 **Minyis**: *Minyae* (Argonauts).
cum picei ... sustulit undam: 'when the pitch-black heavens grew light and flashing lightnings fell in front of the terror-striken ship, and when the yard-arm (*antemna*), dipping to larboard (*laevo / prona*), raised up the gaping water on its point (*cornu*)'. *dehiscentem* refers to the gulfs (or whirlpools) created by the storm in the sea.

625-626 **sed tale fretum**: in their ignorance the Argonauts imagine that this is the usual nature of the sea, not that the winds and storm are abnormal events unleashed by the gods. The Argonauts' inexperience (introduction to this passage) is emphasised.

626-628 **hoc erat ... quod**: 'so this was why our fathers were afraid to profane the forbidden waters with ships'. *rudentibus*: lit. 'with ropes', and so 'with ship's tackle', and hence (part for whole) 'with ships'. For *hoc est quod,* cf. Virgil, *Aeneid* 2.664 whence Valerius probably borrowed it; it is a colloquial usage, found in Plautus.

628-630 **Aegon**: i.e. *mare Aegaeum* (the Aegean).
Cyaneae ... cautes: the 'clashing rocks' (*Symplegades*) at the entrance to the Euxine. Note the 'c' alliteration.

631-632 **terrae**: a bold use - 'dwellers on land'.
sacrosque ... fluctus: 'shun the sacred waves once more (*iterum*)', i.e. return to their former state of innocence and simplicity.

633 **iterant**: 'repeat'.
segni ... leto: '(weeping that they are to meet) a dullard's death'; cf. Lucan 9.849 - *segnia fata* ('a coward's fate').

634-637 **Amphitryoniades**: Hercules (son of Amphitryon).
toti: 'totally sunk in contemplation of their misery'; for this use of *totus*, cf. Horace, *Satires* 1.9.2 - *nescioquid meditans nugarum, totus in illis*; Ovid, *Fasti* 6.251 - *in prece totus eram*.
alnus: 'alder; ship, boat' (cf. passage 5.596 above).

639-642 **subitus trifida Neptunus in hasta**: such use of the

preposition (*in*) is more suitable to referring to garments
in which a person is dressed (e.g. Valerius 1.840 - *seu
venit in vittis castaque in veste sacerdos*) but *in* with
hasta is also found in the sense of 'leaning upon' (Valerius
4.281; 5.462; 8.133). Here he has in mind Virgil, *Aeneid*
5.37 - *horridus in iaculis*; his bold adaptation (*subitus in
hasta*) indicates the suddenness of the theophany; the sea-
god appears, trident in hand, an awesome sight.

9. VALERIUS FLACCUS 2.38-58: NIGHT SCENE AT SEA

If the experience of sea-travel is new to the Argonauts, the
descent of night adds to their apprehension. The stress
placed on pioneering seamanship suggests that the object of
Valerius' poem was perhaps to some extent a glorification of
the emperor Vespasian's achievements in securing Roman rule in
Britain and opening up the sea to navigation, as the Euxine was
opened up by the Argo. In the poem's prologue (1.7-12), appeal-
ing to Vespasian to favour his enterprise, Valerius specifically
refers to this among Vespasian's achievements:

> tuque o pelagi cui maior aperti
> fama, Caledonius postquam tua carbasa vexit
> oceanus Phrygios prius indignatus Iulos,
> eripe me populis et habenti nubila terrae,
> sancte pater, veterumque fave veneranda canenti
> facta virum.

At another level the whole Argonautic quest may be seen as a
legendary reflection of early voyages in search of precious
metals.

In this, their first night at sea, the Argonauts are compared
to a traveller overtaken by night on an unfamiliar road.
Valerius' similes have been carefully studied by Fitch (1976)
and categorised into phrase-similes (without finite verb) and
clause-similes (with finite verb). Apollonius' *Argonautica* has
63 phrase-similes out of a total of 139 similes, Virgil's *Aeneid*
30 out of 135, Ovid's *Metamorphoses* 74 out of 195 and Valerius
only 20 out of 134. The developed clause-simile is character-
istic of high epic and Valerius follows Virgilian practice in
maintaining an atmosphere of seriousness in his similes, to
which his lap-dog simile (7.124-126 - passage 16 below and
n. *ad loc.*) is not to be seen as an exception. However,
Valerius' clause-similes are noticeably brief, about four lines
on average. In this respect he seems to come close to the
practice of Lucan, whose clause-similes average three and a
half lines and whose phrase-similes occur even more rarely than
in Valerius; of 79 similes noted in Lucan by Heitland, no more
than a handful belong to the latter type (Haskins/Heitland
(1887) 84-88). By contrast Statius uses lengthy similes: 49
out of the 217 similes in the *Thebaid* exceed five lines, as

against 3 out of 114 clause-similes in Valerius. Where Statius
and Valerius do concur is in the frequency of similes; both have
one roughly every 45 lines. (On Valerius' similes in general,
see Summers (1894) 59-60.)

The night scene in this passage may be compared and contrasted
with that in Silius Italicus (7.282-307 - passage 18 below).
Sources for the scene, unlike those for the storm, are more
difficult to trace; the subject had hardly become a well-
developed topos. But the opening of this excerpt (38-40)
suggests that Valerius may well have read a poem on Germanicus'
North Sea expedition written by C. Albinovanus Pedo, the sol-
dier poet who was a friend of Ovid (*Epistulae ex Ponto* 4.10).
It is at least interesting to compare our excerpt with some
lines from that poem quoted approvingly by the elder Seneca
(*Suasoriae* 1.15):

> iam pridem post terga diem solemque relictum,
> iamque vident noti se extorres finibus orbis
> per non concessas audaces ire tenebras,
> Hesperii metas extremaque litora mundi;
> nunc illum, pigris immania monstra sub undis   5
> qui ferat, oceanum, qui saevas undique pistres
> aequoreasque canes, ratibus consurgere prensis!
> accumulat fragor ipse metus: iam sidere limo
> navigia, et rapido desertam flumine classem,
> seque feris credunt per inertia fata marinis   10
> quam non felici laniandos sorte relinqui.
> atque aliquis prora caecum sublimis ab alta
> aëra pugnaci luctatus rumpere visu,
> ut nihil erepto valuit dinoscere mundo,
> obstructo tales effundit pectore voces: 15
> 'quo ferimur? fugit ipse dies, orbemque relictum
> ultima perpetuis claudit natura tenebris.
> anne alio positas ultra sub cardine gentes
> atque alium proris intactum quaerimus orbem?
> di revocant, rerumque vetant cognoscere finem   20
> mortales oculos! aliena quid aequora remis
> et sacras violamus aquas, divumque quietas
> turbamus sedes?'

1-7 *vident*: this remains the main verb throughout.
11 *quam non felici ... sorte*: 'by how wretched a fate'.
14 *erepto*: the world has been 'snatched from their sight'.

The influence of Pedo's poem on Tacitus' narrative of the same
expedition by Germanicus (*Annales* 2.23-24) has been suspected
(cf. the end of ch. 24 - *miracula narrabant, vim turbinum et
inauditas volucres, monstra maris, ambiguas hominum et beluarum
formas, visa sive ex metu credita*). Pedo's lines have a unique
interest in that he himself held a high military command on
land during the war. Germanicus twice, in A.D. 15 and 16, em-
barked part of his army, carried it over the North Sea to the
mouth of the Ems, and met with disaster on the return voyages.

If Valerius was aware of Vespasian's North Sea achievements (see above), he could well have had an added interest, through Pedo, in those of Germanicus.

38-40 **hora:** lit. 'hour (of the day)' but 'night' is implied here.

se vertentis Olympi: *Olympus*, here 'sky, heavens' - 'as they saw the face of the heavens turning'.

41-42 **effusis stellatus crinibus aether:** 'the firmament (*stellatus*, lit. 'starred') with streaming tails (*crinibus*) of comets'.

43-47 **utrimque:** in front and behind.

47-50 **Hagniades:** Tiphys (son of Hagnes), the pilot of the Argo.

non hanc ... sine numine pinum / derigimus: *non* is slightly displaced; it goes with *sine numine*.

Tritonia: Pallas (53 below), i.e. Minerva.

erudiit: here with a double accusative (of the person and of the thing taught); cf. Ovid, *Metamorphoses* 8.215 (the first instance of the usage) - *damnosasque erudit artes* (sc. *Icarum*). As often, a more complicated verb (*erudire*) has taken over the construction of a simpler one (*docere*). Statius imitates the usage (*Thebaid* 10.507-508 - *praeceptaque fortia belli / eruidit genetrix*).

saepe ... dignata carinam est: the sense is 'she has often herself deigned to guide our keel with her hand'.

51-54 **experti:** understand *sumus*, and *manum Tritoniae* as the object.

subitus: adjective for adverb (*subito*).

pro: as an interjection, found with a vocative (as here) or an accusative - e.g. *pro deum hominumque fidem*.

decimae cecidit tumor arduus undae: 'the mounting height of the tenth wave has fallen harmlessly'. The ancients believed that every tenth wave was larger than the rest; cf. Ovid, *Metamorphoses* 11.529-530 - *sic ubi pulsarunt celsi latera ardua fluctus, / vastius insurgens decimae ruit impetus undae;* *Tristia* 1.2.50; Lucan 5.672; Silius Italicus 14.122; Seneca, *Agamemnon* 502.

incassum: adverb (also written *cassum*) from the adjective *cassus*, 'empty, hollow' and hence with genitive or ablative, 'devoid of, deprived of, without' or on its own 'vain, futile, useless, fruitless'.

55-58 **quin:** as adverb, 'why not?; how not? (only in exhortation or remonstrance); rather, nay, indeed, in fact' - usually with present indicative to express exhortation (cf. Livy 1.57 - *quin conscendimus equos* - 'let us mount our horses'), but sometimes, as here, with the imperative.

agite: as often no second imperative is added, *agite* having a merely vague adhortatory meaning - 'but come, pull yourselves together!'.

puraque ...: the moon has risen clear (*pura*), her horns not
  heavy (with rain).
nullus in ore rubor: a 'ruddy glow' was thought to be the
  sign of an impending storm (cf. passage 5.546 n. above).
certusque ad talia Titan / integer in fluctus et in uno decidit
  auro: Titan is the Sun; 'and the Sun, a sure guide in res-
  pect of such matters, sank cloudless (*integer*) into the
  waves and in one (blaze of) gold'.

10. VALERIUS FLACCUS 5.416-454: AEETES' PALACE

This passage is an *ekphrasis* (descriptive digression) dealing
with the doors to the palace of king Aeetes of Colchis, father
of Medea and keeper of the Golden Fleece. The original model
for this form of *ekphrasis*, description of a work of art, goes
back to Homer, *Iliad* 18.478ff. (the shield of Achilles) but it
recurs frequently in Hellenistic poetry: e.g. Theocritus 1.29ff.
(a carved drinking-cup); Apollonius Rhodius 1.721ff. (Jason's
cloak); and, with some derivation from Apollonius, Catullus
64.50ff. (an embroidered quilt). In Virgil there are descrip-
tions (the shield of Aeneas (*Aeneid* 8.626-731); and of the
sculptures on the doors of Apollo's temple at Cumae (*Aeneid*
6.14-41 - Appendix passage k below)) which Valerius clearly
took for his model.

The scenes worked by Vulcan on the palace doors of Aeetes
show the 'infancy (*cunabula*) and origin (*ortus*)' of the
Colchian race (417-418), along with the war under king
Sesostris against the Getae, a Thracian tribe, and his eventual
withdrawal of his people, some being sent back to Thebes in
their native Egypt and others settled on the land of Phasis
where he bade them take the name of Colchians (418-422). Next
comes the rape of the nymph Aea by Phasis, the river of Colchis
(425ff.); then Phaethon, son of the Sun-god, who borrowed his
father's chariot for one day but, failing to control the
horses, fell into the river Eridanus (Po). His surviving
sisters were turned into poplars which wept tears of amber
(429ff.). Prophetic representations of the building of the
Argo (435ff.), of the preparation by Medea of poisoned gifts
for Jason's young bride (446ff. - cf. Euripides, *Medea*), and of
the death of the bride and the flight of Medea complete the
series of scenes.

416-418 cunabula: neuter plural noun, lit. 'cradle' - here 'in-
    fancy'; cf. Virgil, *Aeneid* 3.105, where Anchises, having heard
    the Delian oracle's command to the Trojans to seek out their
    'ancient mother', speaks of Crete as *gentis cunabula nostrae*.

418-424 Sesostris: this expedition by the Egyptian king
    Sesostris into Asia is related by Herodotus (2.103), who
    believes that the Colchians originated in Egypt; cf. also
    Apollonius 4.272.

Arsinoen: Arsinoe was a town at the head of the *Sinus Heroo-polites* (now the entrance to the Suez Canal).
tepidaeque ... Phari: 'of warm Pharos'; *tepidus*, 'tepid, warm; cooling, cool; faint, languid'. For Pharos, see passage 7.1 n. above.
pinguemque sine imbribus annum: 'fertile, rainless year'.
carbasa bracis: *carbasus, -i* (feminine) and *carbasa, -orum* (neuter plural), 'linen garment, sail, awning'. *bracae, -arum* (feminine plural) and *braca, -ae* (feminine singular), 'trews, trousers'. They are already changing their native linen clothes for Sarmatian trews. In antiquity trousers were a sign of a less civilised mode of life; e.g. *Gallia bracata* for Transalpine Gaul as opposed to *Gallia togata* for Cisalpine Gaul (on the Italian side of the Alps).
Sarmaticis: Sarmatian, i.e. Slavic - pertaining to people living between the Vistula and the Don rivers, in modern Poland and Russia - a loose geographical reference fully in accord with ancient poetic practice.

425-428 Aean: Aea is an invention of Valerius.
discursibus et iam / deficit: 'and now grows weak through running hither and thither' (to escape Phasis' attentions).
alligat unda: cf. Virgil, *Aeneid* 6.438-439 - *tristisque palus inamabilis undae / alligat.*

429-430 pōpuleae: adjective from *pōpulus, -i* (feminine), 'poplar tree'; this bold expression means 'his sisters who had been turned into poplars'.
ater ... globus: 'the charred (lit. 'black') mass' - i.e. what remained of the incinerated Phaethon.

431-432 iuga ... axem: 'yoke and axle' (of the chariot); cf. Ovid's version of the Phaethon story (*Metamorphoses* 2.316f.).
Tethys: sea-goddess, wife of Oceanus and mother of the sea-nymphs and river-gods.
Pyroenta: one of the four horses of the Sun (Ovid, *Metamorphoses* 2.153).

433-434 quin etiam: regularly marking a climax in an enumeration.
Mulciber: Vulcan.
caelarat: 'had carved'; *caelare*, 'to engrave in relief, chase, carve; to adorn'.

435-436 pinus Pagasaea: *Pagasa, -ae* or *Pagasae, -arum*, was a maritime town in Thessaly, afterwards called Demetrias, where the Argo was built. By a bold use of language Valerius declares that 'the Pagasaean pine is woven by the Argoan axe'.
Argoa: 'proleptic' or anticipatory use of the adjective qualifying *securi*; the action of the axe will eventually produce the ship Argo.
texitur: lit. 'is woven', here used of shipbuilding; cf. Ennius, *Annales* 477 - *campus habet textrinum* ('shipyard') *navibus longis*; Ennius, *Alexander* 69-70 (Warmington (1957) I.242) -

classis cita texitur; Ovid, *Heroides* 16.111f. - *fundatura
citas flectuntur robora naves, / texitur et costis panda
carina suis* (where *citas ... naves* and *texitur* echo Ennius).
Virgil uses *intexere* (*Aeneid* 2.16) for the making of the
Wooden Horse of Troy, being the first to use this particular
compound verb in verse.

437-439 habenas: lit. 'reins', here 'sails'.
notus: 'the south wind'.
Odrysio: 'Thracian' (poetic usage).
phocae: 'seals'.

440-441 trepidi: 'excited'.
regina: Medea.

442-445 urbs: Corinth.
hinc: 'hereafter, next'; Valerius moves to the next scene and it
    is worth noting the economy with which he presents his series
    of tableaux.
gemino circumflua ponto: 'washed round by the waters of two seas'.
cantus taeda pernocte iugales: 'wedding songs with torches that
    burn through the night (from *pernox, -octis*)' at Jason's mar-
    riage to Creusa.
ultrices ... Dirae: 'the avenging Furies'; cf. Virgil, *Aeneid*
    4.473.

446-448 deficit: of Medea's state of mind - 'is distressed'.
paelice: *paelex* = 'concubine, mistress', here 'rival, supplanter'.
donum exitiale: i.e. the poisoned dress; for the same phrase,
    cf. Virgil, *Aeneid* 2.31 (of the Trojan Horse).
ante: adverb.
dequesta: Valerius has coined *dequeri* (a formation parallel
    perhaps to *deplorare*); cf. Statius, *Thebaid* 1.104 - *nŏtos
    dequestus*; 11.627 - *talia dequestus*.

449-451: rutilis: referring to the flames produced by the
    virulent poison.

451-454 Ignipotens: 'the Fire-god'.
quis labor ...: the order is *quis labor (sit) aut quae secet
    aligeris anguibus auras*.
visusque reflectunt: 'turn away their gaze'.

11. VALERIUS FLACCUS 5.329-342: MEDEA'S DREAM

This and the following passages (12-16) are chosen to illus-
trate Valerius' depiction of the gradual growth of Medea's
love for Jason. The depiction owes much to Book 3 of Apollonius'
Argonautica, in which the preoccupation of Greek Alexandrian
literature with psychology and strong states of emotion is
most apparent. But Alexandrian influence is not the whole
story. At Rome dictatorial rule or the threat of it had to

.tent cut people off from many of the active and ex-
interests of life, giving rise to a new interest in the
... life of the individual. This is reflected in the
literature of the Silver Age in the pathological observation
of the younger Seneca (e.g. *de Tranquillitate Animi* 9.2 -
a pioneering analysis of the mental state of boredom) and of
Tacitus (e.g. his portrait of Tiberius); the vivid character-
isation in Martial's epigrams stems from similar preoccupations.
Valerius in his depiction of Medea's love is thus not merely
following Alexandrian procedure but responding to something
inherent in the thinking of his own time.

Love at first sight was an Alexandrian cliché; in Apollonius
Cupid's arrow has immediate and powerful effect upon Medea.
Dido's love for Aeneas is rather more subtly handled but there
is still something of the same abruptness at the start of
Aeneid 4. Valerius, however, concentrates on showing the actual
beginning and early development of love. He is able to do so
by interposing the war against the Scythians in Book 6 which
Medea watches with growing love for Jason. Virgil, too, had
interposed war (the fall of Troy) - and also wanderings -
between the inception of Dido's love in *Aeneid* 1 and its ful-
filment in *Aeneid* 4 but, as Books 2 and 3 are narrated by
Aeneas in the first person, the reader is left very much to
imagine the effect of the narration on Dido and on the growth
of her love. Valerius in third person narrative in Book 6 is
able to return amid the war to Medea's feelings (passages 12
and 13).

In this excerpt Medea has been terrified by a prophetic dream
warning her of separation from her father and evils to come.
She foresees the murders of her brother Absyrtus on the journey
from Colchis and of her own children in Corinth, all by her own
hand. Her dream powerfully and dramatically prefigures the
tragic end to the love affair which is about to begin with the
appearance in her father's palace of Jason.

329-332 forte deum ...: 'it chanced (*forte*) that Medea, fright-
ened by the divine portents in the night, as soon as she per-
ceived that the shadows had been put to flight, having sprung
from her bed (*rapta toris*) was going towards the sun's first
cheering rays (*iubar ad placabile Phoebi*) and the river-
waters which purge (*lustrantia flumina*) the horrors of the
night'. To tell a dream to the sun or wash at dawn in clear
water was considered an effective way of averting evil results
(cf. Aeschylus, *Persae* 201; Sophocles, *Electra* 424; Propertius
3.10.13; Virgil, *Aeneid* 8.68).
placabilis: either 'easily appeased, placable' or '(effective
in) pleasing' - here the latter.

333-335 visa pavens ...: 'she seemed, to her terror, to be
leaving the holy groves of Hecate'. Hecate was a goddess

generally associated with the uncanny and the ghost-world;
she was particularly worshipped at crossroads (hence her
title *Trivia*) which were thought of as haunted places.
Medea was priestess of Hecate and, while Valerius in general
presents Medea as a young and tender girl, he does not omit
the element of witchcraft in her that was part of the
tradition.

336-340 dumque pii petit ora patris: 'while she seeks her
devoted father's presence'; *ora,* lit. 'face'.
stupefacta: understand *est.*
fratre tamen conante sequi: in 8.1-201 Valerius tells how
Jason stole the Golden Fleece with Medea's help and sailed
off with her on the Argo. At Leuce, an island at the mouth
of the Danube, they are overtaken by Medea's brother Absyrtus
and her betrothed lover Styrus (8.217ff.).
mox stare ...: 'then she had seen children stand terrified at
the threat of death (*intenta nece*), and herself as they
trembled (*trementum,* genitive plural dependent on *caede*)
stain (*spargere,* lit. 'sprinkle') her hands with their murder
while tears burst from her eyes' - a prevision of her own
children whom she was destined to murder.

12. VALERIUS FLACCUS 6.575-601: MEDEA ON THE CITY WALLS

King Aeetes agrees to surrender the Golden Fleece if the
Argonauts will fight for him against his Scythian enemies.
Book 6 is taken up with battle scenes and has an 'Iliadic'
quality. In this passage, in particular, Valerius clearly
had in mind Homer's scene (*Iliad* 3.161ff.) in which Helen
watches the fighting from the walls of Troy. As Medea watches
the battles from the walls of Colchis, she finds herself
paying particular attention to Jason. While the Iliadic source
is clear Valerius adds his own psychological insight and also
takes the opportunity to display the erudition typical of
Silver epic (Introduction §§42-43). This he does particularly
in his description of customs, dress and armour. On this last
topic Syme (*Classical Quarterly* 23 (1929) 129-137) sees
Valerius' references to the Sarmatian long lance and coat of
mail (6.231ff.) as perhaps associated with campaigns against
the Sarmatians in A.D. 89 and 92 and thus helping to date the
poem. (On Sarmatian dress, cf. passage 10.424 n. above.)

Valerius is generally realistic in his treatment of the love
affair but, by force of literary convention, he uses super-
natural intervention to bring it about. Juno takes the matter
in hand, disguising herself as Medea's sister Chalciope. The
role, if not the disguise, is the same as that which she had
played in Virgil's handling of Dido and Aeneas in *Aeneid* 4.

575-582 certamina belli: a phrase from Lucretius (1.475),
adopted by Virgil (*Aeneid* 10.146).
Iunone magistra: for Juno's match-making activity, cf. 590ff.

below.

nunc quo diversus abiret: 'now to what other part he would ride off'.

583-586 sisteret: 'bring to a standstill'.
vaga lumina: 'wandering eyes'.
fratris: i.e. Absyrtus.
pacti coniugis: 'her betrothed' (Styrus).

590-591 aspera Iuno: Virgil applies the same adjective to Juno (Aeneid 1.279) who is hostile to the Trojans under Aeneas. It fits Valerius' context less well, for here the goddess bears equal favour towards Jason and Medea.

592-594 qui vellera Phrixi ...: 'who seeks to recover the fleece of his kinsman Phrixus which is his due'.

595-596 Cytaeos: i.e. Colchian.
quantisque insultet acervis: 'over what heaps (of slain) he leaps'.

597-599 dilectaque Phrixo / rura: 'the countryside beloved of Phrixus' - Phrixo, dative of agent. The false Chalciope intends to inflame Medea's feelings by dwelling on Jason's probably imminent departure from the land.

599-601 intendere: here 'to pay attention to'.
campis: 'the battlefield'.
dum datur: 'while it is allowed, possible'.
percurrere: 'to scan, view closely'.

13. VALERIUS FLACCUS 6.752-760: MEDEA'S THOUGHTS OF JASON

After her wearing day on the city walls Medea cannot get Jason out of her mind. These lines end Book 6 on a note of excitement and anticipation, with a simile likening her feelings to the frenzy of a Bacchante.

752 optabilis: 'to be wished for, desirable, welcome'.

755-760 Nyctelii: votaries of Bacchus (cf. Ovid, Ars Amatoria 1.567 - Nycteliumque patrem). Nyctelius is a title of Bacchus whose ceremonies are performed at night (from Greek nyx and perhaps telein) - 'as the Nyctelii in their wild revels (fera ... sacra) for a little while resist (the god)'.
mox rapuere deum ...: 'but presently the Thyiads (female followers of Bacchus) have drunk in their god (i.e. become intoxicated), being ready to undertake at any moment any deed whatever, even in such a state of confusion did Medea return ...'. For Valerius' similes see introduction to passage 9 above; Virgil also compares Dido in love to a Bacchante (Aeneid 4.300ff. - Appendix passage 1 below) but there seems no direct borrowing by Valerius and his point is that Medea's resistance to love

is like that of the devotee to Bacchic frenzy, whereas Virgil
is comparing Dido's fury at Aeneas' suspected desertion of
her to an actual frenzy.
inexpletis ... curis: 'with her love-pangs unsatisfied'; *cura*
is often used, in singular or plural, to mean 'the disquiet
of love'.
quique ... vultus: 'and his face which projects (*superest*)
from his hollow helmet'.

14. VALERIUS FLACCUS 7.1-25: MEDEA'S SLEEPLESS NIGHT

Medea's day on the city walls is succeeded by a sleepless night.
Similarly, Virgil has Dido, after hearing Aeneas' story of the
destruction of Troy and the Trojans' wanderings, on fire with
passion and sleepless (*Aeneid* 4.1-30 - Appendix passage m below).
Virgil is describing a mature woman suddenly stricken with an
overmastering love, Valerius a young girl who, at first, finds
it difficult to analyse her feelings (e.g. 6-7 - *vertere tunc*
varios per longa insomnia questus / nec pereat quo scire malo,
and especially 9ff. with their tone of puzzled innocence.
Valerius' Greek model Apollonius handles the matter more speed-
ily but less subtly (*Argonautica* 4.11ff.).

1-3 soli veniens non mitis amanti: 'coming with no comfort for
the lover alone'.

4-7 et mens incensa tenebris: 'and (when) her imaginings took
fire in the darkness'.
vertere: historic infinitive (also *scire*). *vertere ... questus:*
a bold expression - 'began to brood on various complaints'.

10-11 ante tuos ... vultus: 'before I saw your face'; cf. passage
16.126 - *ante fugam* ('before it flees'), and for comparable use
of *post*, 1.139 - *pulsatque chelyn post pocula (= postquam*
biberunt) Chiron; such abbreviated locution was popular in
Silver Age verse and prose (e.g. younger Seneca, *de Ira* 2.28.6
- *post odium* - 'after at one time hating ...' and 3.37.1 -
post vinum - 'after one has drunk ...').

12-13 tam magno discreta mari: 'separated as I am from you by
so great a sea' - their native lands are far apart and, she
wonders, what good is there in her thinking of him repeatedly
when they are likely never to meet again? Cf. 16 below -
quando domos has ille reviset?

13-14 quid in hospite solo / mens mihi?: 'why do my thoughts dwell
only on the stranger?'

17 Haemonias: Haemonia, poetical name for Thessaly.

18-20 huc: 'to this land (Colchis)'.
sed, sit quoque talis, abito: 'but, even though he is such a
hero, let him depart'; *sit quoque talis* is concessive, lit.

'let him be such (a hero)'. She tries to banish Jason from
her thoughts.

21-25 **totumque experta cubile**: lit. 'having tried the whole of
   her bed' (i.e. so as to settle down if possible and get some
   sleep).
tenui ... Eoo: 'as the morning-star (*Eous*) grows faint (with
   the approach of dawn)'.
remis: 'oars' and here, by metonymy, 'oarsmen'.

15. VALERIUS FLACCUS 7.78-81: THE PERFIDIOUS AEETES

Aeetes fails to honour his agreement to hand over the Golden
Fleece though the Argonauts have fought and prevailed on his
behalf against the Scythians. He lays down a further con-
dition that Jason must yoke the fiery bulls and, having ploughed
the plain of Mars before the city, must sow the dragon's teeth
- a task no mortal man may accomplish safely without super-
natural assistance. Medea is torn between devotion to her
father and love for Jason; love wins and she gives him the
magic drugs by which alone he can perform the new labours.
Valerius dwells in Book 7 and 8 on Medea's *pietas*, her loving
regard for her father. *pietas*, a sense of duty, primarily to
father (and ancestral gods), is a central theme of Virgil's
Aeneid represented by the relationship between father and son
(Anchises and Aeneas), with its implications of loyalty to
patria and to *pater familias*. *pietas* is a peculiarly Roman
quality. Valerius contrives in this respect to turn an eastern
European princess into a Roman girl. This brief extract
sharply emphasises Medea's deep concern for Jason and the start
of the conflict between her feelings for him and her feelings
for her father - a conflict inherent also in the following ex-
cerpt.

80-81 **contremuitque metu ...**: 'and she trembled with fear lest
   the stranger in his ignorance dare to do the deed and, un-
   happy man, imagine he was able to perform it'.

16. VALERIUS FLACCUS 7.103-126: CONFLICT OF FEELINGS

Valerius here presents a sensitive picture of a nervous, un-
certain girl deeply in love, yet with scruples about offending
against family loyalty (*pietas* - see introduction to passage
15 above).

The excerpt contains two similes (see introduction to passage
9 above). The first (111-113) is a mythological comparison in
which Medea is likened to Io. To avoid detection by Juno,
Jupiter turned Io, whom he loved, into a heifer which became
a wanderer, eventually crossing the sea to Egypt where she
regained human form. The story is told in more detail by

Valerius (4.351ff.); it is the subject of an *ekphrasis* concerning a decorated basket carried by Europa in Moschus' Hellenistic Greek poem *Europa* and of a lost poem by Catullus' near contemporary Calvus. The point of the comparison here is that Medea, like Io, will become a sea-borne wanderer.

In the second simile (124-127) Medea is compared with a pet dog sickening for rabies, whimpering before final madness overtakes it and it flees (*ante fugam*) from its mistress all over the house. It has been felt that this simile infringes the high seriousness usual in the subject matter of Valerius' similes. However, it deliberately echoes Virgil (*Aeneid* 7.490 - *ille manum patiens mensaeque adsuetus erili*, of the pet stag whose killing becomes the immediate cause of war between the Latins and Aeneas' Trojans). Bathos was probably not intended by Valerius.

103-106 **deserta:** a bold usage, perhaps meaning that Medea's growing sense of alienation from her family amounts to a kind of desertion of her by them.
sŏlo: 'soil, ground'.

107-108 **tales umeros, ea terga relinquit:** 'such shoulders, such a physique (lit. 'back') does he leave her to remember'; cf. Virgil, *Aeneid* 1.589 - *os umerosque deo similis* (the face and shoulders of the hero Aeneas).

109-110 **illa domum ...:** 'she prays that the house and its very door (*postes*) may move forward somewhat'; i.e. so that she may not lose sight of the departing Jason - a bold, if not exaggerated, turn of thought.

111-113 **qualis ubi:** introducing the Io simile (see introduction to this passage above).
Erinys: the Erinyes were avenging spirits who generally worked by disturbing the mind; the slighted Juno, by way of revenge, sent a gadfly to afflict Io, the effect of which was similar to that brought about by the Erinyes.
Phariae: 'Egyptian' (see passage 7.1-4 n. above).

114-115 **circuit:** 'moves about (restlessly)'.
impendet: 'hovers (by the open doors)'.
melior: 'in more gentle mood'.
Minyas: the Argonauts (cf. passage 8.621 above).

116-118 **solo maeret defecta cubili:** 'mourns exhausted on her lonely couch'. The psychological accuracy in the description of Medea's unsettled behaviour in this whole passage is remarkable.

118-120 **rursusque recedens ...:** 'and again returning she asks how Phrixus came as a stranger and settled in the Aeaean land, and how winged (*aligeri*) serpents snatched Circe away.'

ut: 'how'.

consederit: the expected subjunctive in an indirect question
is followed by an indicative, *rapuere*; for similar mood
variation, cf. 1.278 - *steterit*, 280 - *fugerit*, 281 - *intulit*,
and 282 - *sedit* in Valerius; Propertius 2.14.29-30 - *adspice
quid donis Eriphyla invenit amaris / arserit et quantis nupta
Creusa malis.*

Phrixus ... Circen: Phrixus, son of Athamas and Nephele, escaped
from his stepmother's machinations, with his sister, and fled
through the air to Colchis, where he sacrificed the ram to
Jupiter and gave the fleece to king Aeetes. Circe, daughter
of the Sun and Perse, and sister of Aeetes, was a sea-
nymph famed for her beauty and magic arts, whose haunt was a
fabulous island called Aeaea, later identified, in Italy,
with the promontory of Circeii in Latium. She is a major
figure in Homer's *Odyssey* (10.210ff.). Having murdered her
husband, the prince of Colchis, she was expelled by her sub-
jects and (the reference here) removed by her father to Aeaea.
Medea obliquely approaches the matter of real interest to her
(Jason) by asking about Phrixus and Circe, who were connected
with the story of Colchis.

121-123 visu fruitur: 'gazes at (her companions)'; *frui*, 'to
make use of' as well as 'to enjoy, delight in'.
haeret: 'clings to'.
blandior: 'in a coaxing style'.

124-126 toris: the datives (also *mensae erili*) depend upon
adsueta; *dulcis* qualifies *canis* ('a lapdog').
aegra nova ... futura: 'when already sick with a new plague and
imminent (*futura*) madness'.
ante fugam: 'before it flees'.
totos lustrat queribunda penates: 'roams whimpering (*queribunda*)
through the whole house (*penates*)'. *lustrare:* 'to purify by
expiation' or 'to review, survey, examine; to go over or about,
to traverse'.

17. SILIUS ITALICUS 4.81-87: THE RIVER TICINUS

Hannibal has landed in Italy to the great alarm of the inhabi-
tants. While the Carthaginian leader is courting the favour
of the Gauls of northern Italy, Scipio hurries back from
Marseilles. The action at the river Ticinus (218 B.C.) which
follows is a mere skirmish of advance guards; the succeeding
battles at Trebia (218 B.C.) and Lake Trasimene (217 B.C.)
were disasters for the Romans and culminated in their massive
defeat at Cannae (216 B.C.). Silius' lyrically beautiful few
lines on the river Ticinus are in sharp and no doubt intended
contrast to the horrors that are to come as invader and de-
fender struggle for Italy. They are reminiscent of the topos
or commonplace of the pleasance (*locus amoenus*) which is a
feature of classical poetry. This topos describes a rural place

of calm retreat; the details vary, but very often th[
trees, green sward and a babbling brook (see G. Schö
Locus Amoenus *von Homer bis Horaz* (Heidleberg, 1962); ᴵ. ᴸ.
Rosenmeyer, *The Green Cabinet: Theocritus and the European
Pastoral Lyric* (Berkeley and London, 1969) ch. 9 - 'The
Pleasance').

81 flectit: 'turns his march aside to the waters of the Ticinus'.
   The subject is the elder Scipio.

82-84 caeruleas ... aquas et stagna: hendiadys - 'blue waters and
   pools' for 'pools of blue water'.
turbari nescia: 'unable to be stained / polluted'.
vadoso ... fundo: 'on its shallow bed'.

85-87 vix credas labi: 'you would scarcely believe that it
   moved'.
argutos ... cantus: *argutus* (and *argutiae*) can be used of any-
   thing that makes a sharp impression on the senses - most
   often hearing; cf. Virgil, *Georgics* 1.143 - *arguta serra*
   ('rasping saw'); Cicero, *de Legibus* 1.27 - *oculi arguti*
   ('quick eyes'); Virgil, *Georgics* 3.80 - *argutum caput* ('with
   clear-cut lines', of a horse's head). The elder Pliny
   (*Natural History* 15.18) even uses *argutus* of smell, and
   Palladius (3.25.4) of taste (*argutus sapor*). The metaphorical
   uses denote corresponding ideas: quickness of wit, incisive-
   ness of style, expressiveness in art.

18. SILIUS ITALICUS 7.282-307: A NIGHT SCENE

Hannibal has been caught in a trap by Quintus Fabius Maximus
who later acquired as his agnomen 'Cunctator' ('Delayer')
with reference to his military strategy. Finding sleep im-
possible because of his worry, Hannibal rises and wakes his
brother, Mago; together they make a tour of the camp. This
night scene and a general's restlessness on the eve of battle
perhaps recall Lucan (passage 5 above, 506 n.) and the idea
recurs in Shakespeare's *Henry V* on the eve of Agincourt as
well as the opening of Matthew Arnold's epic fragment *Sohrab
and Rustum*.

282-287 cuncta per ...: 'sleep had lulled (*condere*: 'to hide,
   bury') all things to rest over the earth and the expanse
   of the wide sea'.
at non Sidonium ...: 'his heart anxious (*flagrantia*,
   lit. 'blazing') with care and his watchful fears did not
   allow the Carthaginian leader to enjoy (*haurire*, lit. 'to
   drink') the gifts of drowsy night'. *Sidonius*: 'Carthaginian'.

287-290 fulvi circumdat pelle leonis: 'dons the skin of a
   tawny lion'.
qua super instratos ... ante toros: the lion's skin had served
   as a 'groundsheet' on which his bedding (*toros*) had been laid
   (*instratos*). super: here postponed, governs qua; this use

with the ablative is poetic. *proiectus gramine campi*:
'stretched out on the grass of the plain'. *presserat*: lit.
'had pressed', i.e. 'had lain upon'. *ante*: adverb, redund-
antly used. *toros*: *torus* refers to a plumpness or round
swelling of any kind, hence 'muscle, pillow, cushion, couch,
sofa, bed; bridal-bed, marriage, love-affair; bier; knot on
a garland; bank, mound'.

290-293 nec degener ille / belligeri ritus: *ille* refers to
Mago. *ritus, -us* (masculine): 'religious usage, ceremony,
rite; custom, usage, manner, mode'. *degener*: 'degenerate,
not genuine, unworthy of one's ancestors; unworthy, ignoble,
base' - 'he, not proving unworthy of soldierly custom ...'.
membra iacebat / effultus: 'lay with his limbs resting on ...'.

296-297 telum Baliare: 'Balearic sling'; the Balearic islands
were noted for expert slingers.

299 strato ... dorso: 'with its back covered'; his war-horse
(*sonipes*) was saddled. Both master and beast are prepared
for speedy action (cf. Virgil, *Aeneid* 4.135, of Carthaginian
Dido's horse ready for action).

301-302 heus!: 'hello!' found in Comedy and familiar, intimate
talk, often followed by a jussive or (as here) interrogative
sentence. It is normally used by men - only three times in
Comedy by women (Plautus, *Casina* 165; *Rudens* 413; Terence,
Eunuch 594). It is very rare in epic - only twice in Virgil
(*Aeneid* 1.321 - spoken teasingly by Venus, disguised as a
huntress, to her son Aeneas; and *Aeneid* 7.116 - spoken by
the eager boy Iulus).

303-307 incussa ... planta: Silius probably has in mind an
Homeric scene in which Diomede (surrounded by his sleeping
warriors) is woken by Nestor (*Iliad* 10.157ff.) - 'with a
stamp of his foot recalls (his men lying stretched on the turf)
to their military duties (*castrorum ad munera*)'.
illa senectus: 'that old man'.
fatis ... meis currentibus: '(withstands) the flowing tide of my
fortunes'.

19. SILIUS ITALICUS 10.527-542: FUNERAL PYRES AFTER CANNAE

Cannae, a village on the south bank of the Aufidus in Apulia,
was the scene of Hannibal's great victory in 216 B.C. A Roman
army of 48,000 infantry and 6,000 cavalry under L. Aemilius
Paullus and C. Terentius Varro faced Hannibal's 35,000 infantry
and 10,000 cavalry. The battle is handled by Polybius (3.107-
118) and Livy (22.43-49); Silius' treatment covers 9.278-
10.325.

The tree-felling topos in these lines also appears in Lucan
(see introduction to passage 3 above, parallels cited there

and Appendix passage e below. For a treatment of funeral rites
it is also worth comparing passage 27 below).

527-530 sparsoque ... agmine: the men 'dispersed' to carry out
the task enjoined (munera iussa).

530-532 pōpulus: (feminine); cf. passage 10.429 n. above.

533-534 ferale decus: 'funeral decoration'.

535-539 certamine: 'hastily' (lit. 'by contending with one
another').
munus inane peremptis: 'a tribute which means nothing to the dead'.
officium infelix: (also munus inane) extending and explaining
the action of the sentence funereas ... pyras .. texunt as
internal accusatives in apposition: in building funeral
pyres the men performed a mournful duty and offered a tri-
bute meaning nothing to the slain. This appositional con-
struction appears in Latin first in Sallust (Histories
4.69.8 - Eumenem ... prodidere Antiocho pacis mercedem) but
is Greek in origin (cf. Homer, Iliad 24.735 - ῥίψει χειρὸς
ἑλὼν ἀπὸ Πύργου, λυγρὸν ὄλεθρον; Euripides, Orestes 1105 -
Ἑλένην κτάνωμεν, Μενέλεῳ λύπην πικράν). Silius borrowed the
usage from his great model Virgil (cf. Aeneid 6.222-223 -
pars ingenti subiere feretro, / triste ministerium - see
introduction to passage 27 below; Aeneid 9.52-53 - iaculum
attorquens emittit in auras, / principium pugnae).
stagna in Tartessia: Tartessus (identified by some with the
Tarshish of the Bible), a town on the west coast of Spain,
often used by Latin poets to denote the Far West and the
setting sun.
Titania ... orbita: 'the disc of the moon'; Titanius, 'of or
belonging to Titan, the Sun-god'; Diana, the Moon-goddess,
was his sister, to whom the adjective refers.

540-542 Phaëthontia frena: 'the Phaethontian reins', i.e. 'the
chariot of the Sun'. Phaethon, the son of Helios (the Sun-
god), asked to be allowed to guide his father's solar chariot
for a day. He was, however, too weak to control the immortal
horses which bolted with him, and there was real danger that
the world would be set on fire. But Zeus averted catastrophe
by killing Phaethon with a thunderbolt.

20. SILIUS ITALICUS 13.326-340: DESCRIPTION OF PAN

This description occurs in Silius' narration (13.94-380) of
the recapture by the Romans in 211 B.C. of Capua which had
revolted to Hannibal in 216 B.C. The violent impulse of the
victorious Roman soldiers to raze the walls and burn the city
was mysteriously stilled by divine intervention: 'a merciful
god made his way by slow degrees into their inmost hearts.
Unseen by anyone, he (i.e. Pan) taught them all that Capys
had laid the foundations of that proud city in ancient times,
and explained that it was expedient to leave human dwellings

for that vast extent of plain' (13.319-324). There is some-
thing quaint and unexpected about the appearance of Pan at
this historical juncture, an impression heightened by the
poet's comic naivety of description, especially 339-340.
Silius may have wished to repeat the effect in Herodotus
(6.105.2-3) where Pan appeared to the courier Pheidippides
sent from Athens to solicit Spartan help when the Persians
landed at Marathon in 490 B.C. (Though Pan's alleged part
in the story seems doubtful, Pheidippides' feat in covering
roughly 150 miles in two days need not be fictitious.) Alter-
natively, Silius' appearance of Pan may go back to an old
Italian legend.

Pan was a god native to Arcadia and traditionally associated
with herds; his name, if derived from the root seen in the
Latin *pa-sco*, meant 'Feeder' (i.e. herdsman); cf. 342 - *pascua*
('pasture-lands'). Silius may have been familiar with paintings
or mosaics depicting Pan and probably based his description on
such artistic representations.

326-328 Iove ... servari tecta volente / Troïa: 'Jupiter wishing
that the dwellings of the Trojan city should be saved ...',
referring to Capys, a Trojan and legendary founder of Capua.
pendenti similis: 'like one standing on tiptoe'; cf. *pedem
suspendere*, 'to walk on tiptoe'.
imo: with *cornu*, i.e. the bottom of his hoof (he was half-man
and half-goat); 'scarcely leaving any print upon the ground
with his horny hoof'.

329-330 dextera lascivit ... per compita coetu: 'his right hand
plays with a lash of Tegean goat-skin (lit. 'a slain Tegean
she-goat'), dealing sportive blows among the festive crowd at
the cross-ways'. *Tegeatide*: adjective from *Tegea* in Arcadia
(the native region of Pan). At the *Lupercalia*, a Roman festi-
val in honour of Pan held every year on 15 February, priests
(called *Luperci*) ran through the city whipping people whom
they encountered with strips of goat-skin.

331-333 pinus: a regular attribute of Pan (cf. Ovid, *Metamorphoses*
1.699 - *Pan videt hanc, pinuque caput praecinctus acuta / talia
verba refert*; and 14.638 - *pinu praecincti cornua Panes*).

334-335 deo: dative of the person interested.

336-338 in praeruptum tam prona: 'so steep'; *praeruptus* and
pronus convey the same sense, creating extra emphasis.
librans corpus similisque volanti: 'balancing his body on it
like a flying thing'. For *similis volanti*, cf. *pendenti
similis* (327 above).

339-340 interdum inflexus ...: 'sometimes having turned round (*in-
flexus*) he looks and laughs at the antics of the bushy tail
growing behind him'. Though grammatically *nascentia* goes with

ludibria, in sense it is to be taken with *caudae*. *medio* ...
tergo: an odd expression, presumably 'up the middle of his
back'.

21. SILIUS ITALICUS 13.806-822: ROLL-CALL OF ROMAN HEROINES

After the defeat and death of his father and uncle in Spain
(13.381-384), Scipio descends to the underworld to meet the
spirits of his kinsmen (385-396). He sees the ghosts of
famous men and women in Hades and the Sibyl, his guide,
finally predicts the death of Hannibal (397-893). Silius
has set out to recall from *Aeneid* 6 Aeneas' descent to Hades,
his meeting with his father Anchises, and his preview of the
great figures of Roman history. In Virgil (*Aeneid* 6.426ff.)
Aeneas encounters four groups of the untimely dead, the last
one of which consists of women who have died for their love
(including Dido who committed suicide at the end of *Aeneid* 4
because of her fruitless passion for Aeneas). Virgil had drawn
on Homer (*Odyssey* 11.225ff.) where Odysseus in the underworld
saw a long procession of heroines; but Virgil was much more
compact, introducing (*Aeneid* 6.445ff. - Appendix passage n
below) only seven heroines, all victims of bizarre forms of
durus amor and all carefully chosen to lead appropriately
to Dido (see Austin (1977) line 449 n.). By contrast, there
is no deep symbolic or poetically allusive rationale behind
Silius' choice of women; they are simply eminent heroines in
Roman legend. This excerpt is drawn from the beginning of the
scene and is sufficient to suggest the flavour of the whole
(806-850).

806-808 vultus ... traxit: lit. 'Lavinia having been pointed
out drew his gaze'. Lavinia was daughter of king Latinus
and became wife of Aeneas.
virgo: i.e. the Sibyl, Scipio's guide.
lux alma: 'the dawn'; *almus*, 'nourishing, kind, gracious,
bountiful, sweet' - a poetic epithet often used of Ceres,
Venus, and other patron deities of the earth, of light (as
here), day, wine, etc.

809-810 nurus: 'daughter-in-law'; Venus, as Aeneas' mother, was
Lavinia's mother-in-law.
Troiugenas ... Latinis: Aeneas came to Latium as a Trojan and
founded a new stock.

811 thalamos ... Quirini: *thalamus*, 'bedchamber; women's apart-
ment, bridal bed, marriage; dwelling, habitation, abode' and
here 'wife of Quirinus'. *Quirinus* was the name given to
Romulus when deified.

812-815 Hersiliam: Hersilia, wife of Romulus, acted as peace-
maker in the war which arose from the rape of the Sabine women.
gens vicina: i.e. the Sabines.

procos: 'suitors'.
pastori rapta marito: 'carried off by a shepherd-bridegroom';
  pastori (with *marito* in apposition) is dative of agent.
pressit: 'lay upon'.
torum: the bed consisted of scattered straw (*fultum*, lit.
  'supported, sustained, upheld', from *fulcio, fulcire, fulsi,
  fultum; stramen, - inis* (neuter): 'litter, straw, some-
  thing strewn'; *culmus, -i* (masculine): 'stalk, straw').

816 aspice Carmentis gressus: 'see the movements of Carmentis',
  i.e. 'see where Carmentis approaches ...'. Carmentis was
  mythologically a prophetess and mother of Evander (*Evandria
  mater*), the first settler at the site of Rome (cf. Virgil,
  Aeneid 8).

816-817 vestros: i.e. 'Roman'; the Sibyl is addressing Scipio,
  saying that as a prophetess (*praesaga*) Carmentis 'touched
  upon (*tetigit*) your present troubles' (i.e. the struggle
  against Hannibal).

818-820 vis: understand *spectare*; 'do you wish to see what
  appearance Tanaquil has?' (cf. 811 above).
Tanaquil: wife of Tarquinius Priscus, traditionally fifth king
  of Rome (616-579 B.C.) and of Etruscan origin; it was believed
  by the Romans that he brought Etruscan customs, cults, and
  craftsmen to Rome. For Tanaquil's prophetic power cf. Livy
  1.34.8 - *ibi ei (Tarquinio) carpento sedenti cum uxore aquila
  suspensis demissa leniter alis pilleum aufert, superque
  carpentum cum magno clangore volitans rursus, velut ministerio
  divinitus missa, capiti apte reponit, inde sublimis abit.
  accepisse id augurium laeta dicitur Tanaquil, perita, ut vulgo
  Etrusci, caelestium prodigiorum mulier*. Horace perhaps had
  this scene in mind in *Odes* 1.34.14ff. - *hinc apicem rapax /
  Fortuna cum stridore acuto / sustulit, hic posuisse gaudet*.
dextros agnovit in alite divos: 'recognised in the
  flight of a bird that the gods were favourable (*dextros*)';
  dexter and *sinister* belong to the language of augury (*augurium*),
  an Etruscan form of divination involving the observation and
  the interpretation of the number, species, flight, cries,
  feeding-habits, and other symbolic acts of birds.

821-822 pudicitiae Latium decus: 'the glory of Roman chastity';
  Latium is transferred epithet.
inclita leti: 'famous for her death'; the genitive (*leti*) is a
  poetic usage; *inclitus* (more commonly *inclutus*) is ante-clas-
  sical and poetic. Lucretia, wife of Tarquinius Collatinus,
  was raped by Sextus, son of Tarquinius Superbus, and having
  told her husband, committed suicide; the incident led to a
  popular uprising under Junius Brutus against the Tarquins and
  to their expulsion from Rome (Livy 1.57-59; Ovid, *Fasti* 2.721-
  852).

22. SILIUS ITALICUS 16.229-244: SCIPIO AND SYPHAX

Scipio had crossed from Spain to Africa to secure alliance with
Syphax, king of Numidia, against Carthage. The mission is
historical fact but the scene in this excerpt is imaginatively
and charmingly set by Silius in the palace of Syphax. Scipio
rises from his bed before sunrise and goes to visit the young
king whom he finds playing with his pet lion-cubs. In the
lines which follow our extract Syphax generously expresses
high regard for his Roman guest and gladly forms the alliance.

229-234 pariebat: 'was bringing forth (a new day)'; the metaphor
  is from childbirth. For the language cf. Virgil, *Aeneid*
  6.255 - *ecce autem primi sub limina solis et ortus.*
stabulisque ... solis equi: 'the steeds of the sun were ap-
  proaching (*subibant*) their yokes from their stables'.
axem: 'axle-tree' and, by synecdoche ('part for the whole'), 'car,
  chariot'.
Massyli: *Massylus* or *Massylius* (adjective), 'African'.

235-236 mos patrius: 'ancestral custom, custom of the country'.
alendo: 'by cherishing them'.

237-238 fera ... ora: 'their dreadful muzzles'.

239-242 decus: here 'sceptre'.
de more: 'in customary fashion'.

23. STATIUS, *THEBAID* 2.496-526: AN AMBUSH

This passage is based (with characteristically Statian touches)
on the scene in Virgil (*Aeneid* 11.522ff. - Appendix passage p
below) where Turnus, having gratefully accepted the aid of the
warrior-queen Camilla, asks her to engage the enemy cavalry
while he lays an ambush for Aeneas and his infantry. Here the
ambush is prepared for Tydeus, ally of Polynices, as he returns
from an embassy to Thebes where Polynices' brother Eteocles is
exercising the first period of rule in what was agreed would be
an alternating system. Tydeus emerges victorious and returns
safely to Polynices in Argos. Statius' description of the scene,
with its elaborate digression on the Sphinx and its end,
is rather baroque and overdrawn by comparison with that of
Virgil.

The passage in *Aeneid* 11 may be compared with Livy's descrip-
tion of the Caudine Forks (9.2.6f.), and the words *densis* ...
latus are repeated from *Aeneid* 7.565-566. In Virgil there is
a 'valley with hidden recesses' (*curvo anfractu valles*) and
a 'hidden plateau' (*planities ignota*) lying 'amid the watch-
towers of the mountain-top' (*in speculis summoque in vertice
montis*). Statius uses similar wording but a different and
somewhat obscure picture emerges: his hills are darkened by

the shadow of a mountain which overtops them (*superni / montis*) and of the trees on the ridges.

496-497 per dumos: 'through thickets'.
praecelerant: 'they hurry forward'; the prefix intensifies the sense.
legunt compendia: 'they chose the shorter way'; i.e. they take a short cut through the dense woods.

498-504 lecta dolis sedes: 'a choice place for a stratagem', 'a place just made for an ambush'.
gemini procul urbe ...: 'two hills near the city press hard upon one another with an evil gulf (*malignis / faucibus*) between them', thus creating a narrow pass in which an ambush may easily be arranged (hence *malignis* with its sense of the sinister).
insidias natura ...: 'nature has implanted treachery (*insidias*) in the place and a secret means (*caecam opem*) of lying hidden'.
arte: an adverb.
devexa ... arva: 'sloping fields'.

504-505 importuna crepido: *crepido,* 'a pedestal, base for statue' or 'mound, pier, mole, dam, shore, bank, a high projection'; here 'a threatening cliff'.
Oedipodioniae domus alitis: 'the home of the winged monster of Oedipus'; i.e. the Sphinx, defeated by Oedipus who solved its riddle.

505-512 hic fera quondam ...: 'here once upon a time she stood fiercely uplifting (*erecta* - middle use of participle) her pallid cheeks and her eyes stained with putrid matter (*tabum, -i*, neuter), her feathers clotted with abominable gore; grasping human remains (*virum = virorum*) and pressing to her bare breast half-eaten bones she scanned (*conlustrat*) the plains with fearful gaze in case a stranger should dare to join in the strife (*concurrere*) of riddling words (*dictis ... inexplicitis*) or a traveller come to grips with her (*comminus ire*) and have speech with her as her tongue uttered fearful things'.
tremendo: an emendation by Müller; the manuscripts have either *frementi* or *trementi*.

513-515 strictosque in vulnera dentes: 'her teeth bared (lit. 'drawn', like swords) for making wounds'. Housman emended *fractos* of the manuscripts to *strictos*, which yields better sense.
adplausu: i.e. by the beating of her wings.
circum hospita ... ora: 'round about the faces of the strangers'; *hospita*: from the adjective *hospitus*, either 'hospitable' or 'strange, foreign'.

516-518 et latuere doli: i.e. her riddle was not solved. Cf. Virgil, *Aeneid* 1.130 - *nec latuere doli.*

simili deprensa viro: 'caught by a hero (i.e. Oedipus) who was well matched with her'. *viro*: dative of agent.

inexpletam ... alvum: 'her insatiable belly'; for *inexpletus* = *inexplebilis,* cf. Virgil, *Aeneid* 8.558-559 - *Euandrus dextram complexus euntis / haeret inexpletus lacrimans*; Ovid, *Metamorphoses* 3.439 - (of Narcissus) *spectat inexpleto mendacem lumine formam*; also Seneca, *Epistulae Morales* 89.22 - *stomachus inexplebilis.*

519-520 monstrat silva nefas: signs of the foul story are still found in the wood.

damnatis: by poetical transference, for *damnosis,* 'injurious, baneful'.

521-523 non Dryadum ...: i.e. the dancing troops of wood-nymphs take no delight in the place.

Faunorum: Faunus, son of Picus, grandson of Saturn, and father of Latinus (king of Latium) introduced tillage and grazing, and after death was the protecting deity of agriculture and shepherds. He was identified with Pan, and, by assimilation, the plural *Panes* (cf. passage 20.331 n. above) gave rise to a plural *Fauni* ('woodland spirits'). For *Fauni* and *Dryades* together, cf. Virgil, *Georgics* 1.10-11 - *et vos, agrestum praesentia numina, Fauni / ferte simul Faunique pedem Dryadesque puellae.*

dirae ... volucres: i.e. vultures.

523-526 acti / deveniunt peritura cohors: a construction 'according to sense'; i.e. plurals *acti* and *deveniunt* are followed by a singular collective subject *cohors. acti*: 'speeding' (lit. 'driven on'). *peritura*: i.e. destined to fall to Tydeus' sword.

adnixi iaculis: 'leaning on their spears'.

coronant: for this sense ('surround'), cf. Virgil, *Aeneid* 9.380 - *omnemque aditum custode coronant* (which Statius seems to have had in mind).

24.   STATIUS, *THEBAID* 3.420-439: RUMOUR

War has been decided upon at Argos; Polynices will seek to wrest the kingship of Thebes from his brother Eteocles. Mars (420 - *deus armifer*) is pictured driving his chariot through the heavens as a dramatic indication of impending war. He is accompanied by allegorical personifications, *Furor, Ira, Pavor* and, described in more detail, *Fama.* For such personifications, see Introduction §26; Statius was particularly fond of them. *Fama* had been described by Virgil (*Aeneid* 4.173-188 - Appendix passage c below) but in a rather different context - spreading the news of the love affair of Dido and Aeneas - and with different description. Statius seems to have deliberately created his own version of *Fama* but he makes one verbal concession to Virgil, perhaps to indicate his awareness of the passage he is challenging (see 430 n. below).

Statius' imagery is somewhat similar to that of the *Book of Revelation* (e.g. ch. 6). The latter's date of composition is uncertain: some associate it with the persecution of Christians under Nero in A.D. 65; but it is more probably related to a later persecution under Domitian in A.D. 96, which would make it contemporary with the *Thebaid*. Points of similarity in apocalyptic language (cf. St. Luke 21.25-27) between the two works provide an interesting comparison, though they are doubtless coincidental.

The extract contains an extended simile in which Mars is compared to the sea-god Neptune. The disparity between the descriptions of Mars, with allegorical personifications on his errand of destruction, and Neptune, with his personified winds, is hardly great enough to give real force and point to the simile.

420-424 desuper: 'from on high'.
Taenarium cacumen: 'the height of Taenarum' (in Laconia), near which was a cavern, a legendary entrance to the underworld.
Therapnas: Therapnae (or Therapne), also in Laconia, was the birth-place of Helen who was worshipped there together with her brothers Castor and Pollux (the Dioscuri) and Menelaus. Why Statius connects it with Apollo (*Apollineas*) is not clear.

424-425 comunt Furor Iraque cristas: 'Fury and Anger arrange his crest'; for personification in Statius and elsewhere, see Introduction §26.

425-429 at vigil omni / Fama ...: 'but Rumour, alive to every sound, and girt about with empty tidings of approaching war (*tumultus*), flies in front of his chariot and, urged on by the breath of his snorting winged steeds, with muffled murmuring flaps out her trembling plumage'.

429-431 auriga: 'the charioteer', probably Bellona, goddess of war and sister of Mars (cf. *Thebaid* 7.73), unless the action of *Pavor* (425 - *frena ministrat*) is that of a charioteer.
facta, infecta loqui: cf. Virgil, *Aeneid* 4.190 - (also of *Fama*) *et pariter facta atque infecta canebat*.
pater: Mars himself.
increpat: 'harries'.

432-434 qualis ubi: 'just as when ...'. For the prison in which Aeolus kept the winds, cf. Virgil, *Aeneid* 1.50ff.

434-437 tristis comitatus: (singular) 'a gloomy company', i.e. the *Nimbi, Hiemes, Nubila* and *Tempestas* who form the plural subject for *fremunt*.
eunti: dative of the person interested - 'in his train'.

437-439 Cyclades: Delos was formerly a floating island, but when Leto was due to give birth to Apollo and Artemis there, it became stationary, fastened to the islands of Myconos and

Gyaros.
magnique *iidem testaris alumni*: 'and call upon the protection
of your great nursling (Apollo)' - an allusive turn typical
of Statius.

25.   STATIUS, *THEBAID* 4.786-796:   THE CHILD OPHELTES IN THE MEADOW

There are in the whole range of Latin poetry few passages which
surpass this in its tender quality. Statius seems to have had
a special interest in children: cf. the death of Opheltes from the
bite of a snake (5.499-753) and the funeral rites held for him
(6.1-248 - see passage 27 below), and three *epicedia* (mourn-
ing poems) in memory of children (*Silvae* 2.1; 2.6; 5.5), and the
reference e.g. to the deep relaxed sleep of childhood (*Achil-
leid* 1.229 - *qui pueris sopor*). The relationship of mother/
son also attracted Statius: in the *Thebaid* Atalanta and
Parthenopaeus; Ismenis and Crenaeus; and Ino and Palaemon;
Thetis and Achilles in the *Achilleid*. This is in contrast with
Virgil who stressed the father/son relationship: Anchises and
Aeneas; Aeneas and Iulus (Ascanius); Evander and Pallas.

786-793 *faciles sternit procursibus herbas*: 'crushes the soft
grass as he crawls forward'.
lactis egeno / ... plangore: i.e. his cry expresses his need
for milk.
patulo trahit ore diem: 'drinks in the day with open mouth'.

794-796 *sic tener ...*: 'such was the young Mars (*Mavors*) amid
the Odrysian (Thracian) snow, such the winged boy (Cupid) on
the heights of Maenalus (in Arcadia), such was the naughty
Apollo when, creeping on the shore of Ortygia (Delos), he
set the island's side atilt'. Apollo's divine weight upsets
the balance of Delos (on weight as an attribute of divinity,
cf. passage 1.55 n. above). Statius apparently thinks of
Delos as anchored, not grounded (see passage 24.438 n. above).
These lines, with their apparently tasteless mythological
intrusion, contrast adversely with the preceding delicate
observation.

26.   STATIUS, *THEBAID* 5.361-375:   A STORM AT SEA

This excerpt is from a long digression (*Thebaid* 5.17-498)
which narrates the story of Hypsipyle, queen of Lemnos, whose
population, entirely of women, entertained the Argonauts *en
route* for Colchis (the tale also appears in Apollonius and
Valerius Flaccus). Within sight of land the Argo is assailed
by a storm of unusual violence. This storm at this point in
the Argonaut story seems to be an addition by Statius but he
takes the opportunity to handle a stock epic theme which he
embroiders in his own particular way. For discussion of the
storm topos, see introduction to passage 5 above and Appendix

passage g below.

361-364 quantum Cortynia currunt / spicula: '(and they were al-
ready distant from the land) the range of Cretan arrows';
Crete was famous for its archers.
sistit agens: 'bringing (a cloud heavy with dark rain) he set
it (*sistit*) over the very rigging (*ipsa armamenta*) of the
Pelasgian vessel (Argo)'.

364-366 dies: here 'daylight' (a not uncommon sense).
quis: = *quibus*, dative with *concolor* ('of the same colour');
the wave takes on the colour of the dark sky.

366-372 obnixi: 'striving'.
diripiuntque fretum: 'and they rend the sea'.
umida tellus: 'the wet sand (lit. 'earth')'.
nigris ... verticibus: 'in black eddies'.
totumque ... pendet: 'and the whole sea hangs poised between the
conflict of the winds (*notis*, lit. 'south winds')'.
arquato ... dorso: 'with its back arched until it almost (*iamiam*)
touched the stars'. The series of individually striking
phrases, concentrating the focus of stylistic attention on the
single phrase, is very much a feature of Statius (and the
younger Seneca), in contrast with Lucan who works with larger
units.
incertae ... alno: 'nor does the buffeted (*incertae* - it does not
know where it is going to go next under the impact of the
storm, cf. passage 5.552) craft any longer have its former
motion (*impetus*)'. *alno*: see passage 5.596 n. above.

372-375 flagellat: lit. 'flogs', but here 'causes (the ship)
to heave and sway'; cf. *Thebaid* 3.36-37 - *ima flagellatis ...
ponderibus trepidavit humus* ('the earth with heaving masses
trembled to its foundations').
arbor: here 'mast'.

27. STATIUS, *THEBAID* 6.54-73: FUNERAL RITES

The funeral pyre of the young Opheltes (see passage 25 above)
is described. In the *epicedia* (funeral songs) of the *Silvae*,
Statius followed the example both of the philosophical consol-
ation (e.g. Seneca, *ad Marciam*) and of funeral speeches and
consolatory addresses practised in the rhetorical schools,
dividing them into regular parts - praise of the dead person,
description of his last illness and death, the funeral, arrival
in the underworld, etc. He has references to cremation ritual:
Silvae 2.1.181ff. - the pyre of Opheltes (in a poem to Atedius
Melior on the death of a foster-son); *Silvae* 3.3.33-37 - the
pyre of Claudius Etruscus (whose son Statius is seeking to
console).

The present passage may be compared with Silius 10.527ff. (pas-
sage 19 above) which leads (561ff.) to the cremation of Paulus.

The main source is provided by Virgil, *Aeneid* 6.212-235
(Appendix passage q below), in which the Trojans make a great
pyre for Misenus and the funeral rites are carried out with
close attention to detail (Austin (1977) *ad loc.*; and cf.
Aeneid 11.64ff.; 184ff.). Virgil's description gives evidence
for the most elaborate kind of Roman funeral ceremony. It
looks back to Homer's funeral of Patroclus (*Iliad* 23.109ff.)
but its ethos is entirely Roman, involving deep solemnity in
keeping with a final act of *pietas*. Its position, immediately
before Aeneas' descent to the underworld to visit his father,
gives it a special relevance within Virgil's central theme of
pietas. (For Roman funerary rites in general see J. M. C.
Toynbee, *Death and Burial in the Roman World* (London, 1971)
43ff.; and for Virgil's description in particular, C. Bailey,
Religion in Virgil (Oxford, 1935) 287ff.)

Statius' passage, compared with that of Virgil, well illustrates
the former's rather baroque taste and tendency towards elabor-
ation of detail.

54-56 **interea**: often used in Latin poetry to mark a change of
  scene.
tristibus ... ramis teneraque cupresso: hendiadys, with trans-
  position of adjectives; *tristis* refers in a sense to the
  cupressus, and *tener* to the *rami* (*teneri rami*: 'young pliant
  shoots'). The cypress was much associated with mourning.
  teneraque cupresso: cf. Virgil, *Georgics* 1.20 - *teneram ...*
  cupressum.
damnatus flammae torus: i.e. a funeral bier destined to be con-
  sumed in the flames.
ima virent agresti stramina cultu: truncated locution, typical
  of Statius; 'at the bottom are laid green foliage and branches
  taken from the countryside'. *stramen* from *sternere*, anything
  spread under something else. Cf. Virgil, *Aeneid* 11.67 (of Pal-
  las and his bier) - *hic iuvenem agresti sublimem stramine ponunt.*

57-58 **operosior**: understand *est.*
morituris: an added touch of pathos; flowers were a symbol of
  mortality from Homer onwards, e.g. *Iliad* 8.306 - '(a dying
  man) bowed his head to one side like a poppy that in a garden
  is laden with its fruit and the rains of spring'.

59-61 **Arabum strue**: = *acervo odoramentorum Arabicorum*; 'third
  in order is raised up a heap of Arabian spices ...'.
incana ... tura: *in-*.is intensive ('very hoary'). *glebis*: 'in
  lumps'; *glaeba* (the more usual form), 'clod; earth; lump'.
ab antiquo durantia cinnama Belo: periphrasis for *perantiqua.*
  Belus was in myth a king of Egypt, or founder of the
  Assyrian empire (cf. Virgil, *Aeneid* 1.621; Ovid, *Metamorphoses*
  4.213).

62-65 **summa crepant auro ...**: 'the summit rustles with gold foil,
  and a soft cloth dyed with Tyrian purple is raised up to lie
  on the top; polished gems throw light upon it at every point,
  and within a border (*medio*, see below) of acanthus Linus is

woven along with the hounds which caused his death'.

supercilium: 'eyebrow' and so 'severity, sternness, austerity' or 'pride, haughtiness' and then 'ridge, summit of a hill' (cf. Livy 34.29 - *supercilium tumuli*) - here in the sense of 'that which lies on top'.

medio ... acantho: intensive use of *medius* (cf. Catullus 64.149 and C. J. Fordyce (ed.) *ad loc.*); here in the sense of 'surrounding'.

intertextus: cf. Virgil, *Aeneid* 8.167 - *chlamydemque auro dedit intertextam*; Ovid, *Metamorphoses* 6.128 - *flores hederis habet intertextos*.

Linus: the version of the legend current at Argos made him the baby son of Apollo and Psamathe, a local princess, who exposed him; he was killed by hounds, and the city plagued by his father Apollo until appeasement was made (Pausanias 1.43.7-8). The story is told in *Thebaid* 1.557ff.

67-71 gloria: (with *ambitus*) subject of *circumdat*; the 'chequered fame' (*gloria mixta malis*) and 'pride' (*ambitus*) of the family cause them to build up the pyre with arms and the spoils of ancestors 'as though (*ceu*) there were being borne forth to the funeral the body of a great hero (*grande onus*) and to the pyre the limbs of a mighty warrior', whereas it is, in fact, the funeral of a small boy.

parvique ... manes: 'the infant shade (*manes*) is magnified by the pomp (*funere*)'.

72-73 miseranda voluptas: oxymoron; Statius often remarks that there is pleasure in mourning, e.g. *Thebaid* 12.45 - *amant miseri lamenta malisque fruuntur*; 12.793-794 - *gaudent lamenta novaeque / exsultant lacrimae*.

muneraque ... annis graviora: the gifts are greater than would seem fitting for the funeral of a child.

28. STATIUS, *THEBAID* 8.373-394: INVOCATION OF THE MUSE

This excerpt is drawn from the opening of a long section of the epic which is devoted to the exploits and death of Tydeus. As he begins upon this fresh topic, Statius solicits the aid of the Muse, Calliope. Such invocations had become common epic practice, not only at the start of the poem but at significant points of departure into new subjects within it. Homer asked for the Muse's support not only at the start of the *Iliad* and *Odyssey* but also when he begins his 'catalogue of ships' (*Iliad* 2.484ff.) and, as the poet was seen as the instrument through whom the divine Muses mediated their poetry to men, the practice became a standard topos.

Virgil appeals to the Muse at the outset of his epic (*Aeneid* 1.8ff.) and again, specifically to Erato, in the exordium to the second half (*Aeneid* 7.37ff.) where he switches to the topic of the fight for Italy. Again he makes such an appeal at a

crucial moment in the narrative (*Aeneid* 6.264ff.) when Aeneas
enters the underworld, praying for the spirits' leave to reveal
their secrets; and the technique is elsewhere in the *Aeneid*:
7.641ff. (before the list of Italian troops); 9.525ff. (before
Turnus' heroic actions); 10.163ff. (before the catalogue of
Aeneas' ships); 12.500ff. (before the exploits of Turnus and
Aeneas).

The challenge of these Virgilian passages was noted by Silver
epic poets who duly inserted invocations to the Muses at suitable
points (cf. Statius, *Thebaid* 1.3ff.; Valerius Flaccus 3.213ff.,
6.34ff., and 516ff.; Silius Italicus 1.3ff., 3.222ff., 12.390ff),
though Lucan ignores the convention in conformity with his
abandonment of divine intervention. Horace, *Satires* 1.5.53ff.,
parodies the manner. See Austin (1971) 8-11 n. *ad loc.*

373-374 alias nova suggere vires: 'supply fresh strength from
 a new source'.
Calliope: chief of the Muses and patron divinity of epic poetry.
chelyn: 'tortoise-shell lyre' - *chelys* (feminine), Greek for
 tortoise; Hermes made the first lyre by stretching strings on
 the shell.

375-381 ultro: 'of their own accord'.
fruitur caelo: 'enjoys the air of heaven'.
bellatoremque: this noun takes the place of an adjective (qualify-
 ing *campum*); cf. Virgil, *Georgics* 2.145 - *bellator equus*; also
 Aeneid 9.721 - *bellator deus* (of Mars); *Aeneid* 12.614 - *bella-
 tor Turnus*.
nigroque ... hiatu: 'with black-gaping jaws'.
nil vulgare legens: 'choosing nothing common'. He marks with
 bloodstained nail as victims (*funera*) those most worthy to
 live, being in their prime (*praecipuos*) of years and courage
 (*animis*).

381-382 Sororum: the *Parcae* or Fates, three sisters (*Sororum*),
 controlling each person's life and fortune: Lachesis assigns
 the lot, Clotho spins the thread of life (*pensum* and *licia*,
 'threads'), and Atropos severs it.
Furiae: Furies or avenging deities, here associated with the
 furor or madness of war which destroys the fittest and the
 most valiant.

383-385 Bellipotens: 'the War-god'.

386-389 amor: with both *patriae* and *lucis*.
animusque ultra thoracas anhelus / conatur: 'and their panting
 courage strives beyond their breastplates'.

390-394 cornipedes: 'horn-footed steeds' - rare before Statius,
 but used often as a noun by him and by Silius; cf. passage
 31.155.
ceu mixti ...: 'as though (*ceu*) they have been made one (*mixti,*

understand *sint*) with their masters and have put on (*induerint*)
their riders' wrath'.
equitesque supinant: 'throw the horsemen backward'.

29. STATIUS, *THEBAID* 8.548-553: A POET'S DEATH

These lines from a battle scene form a neat epitaph for Corymbus,
a minor warrior and poet who dies fighting on behalf of Thebes.
In his desire to sing of *pugnasque virosque* he is a prototype of
the epic poet; see Vessey (1973) 289.

548-551 Heliconius: adjective from Helicon, the largest mountain
   in Boeotia which was traditionally the haunt of the Muses - so
   a suitable designation for a poet.
Stygii ... pensi: *pensum* (from *pendere*, to weigh), 'portion (of
   wool) weighed; day's work, task'; here the thread of mortal
   life spun by the Fates. *Stygii*: belonging to the Styx, a
   river in the underworld - so 'deadly, fatal'.
positis ... astris: either 'citing the stars' or 'by the position
   of the stars'.
Uranie: the Muse of heavenly lore - hence 'the teacher of astro-
   logy'.

551-553 pugnasque virosque: cf. Virgil, *Aeneid* 1.1 - *arma
   virumque* (of his epic subject matter).
amissum ... sorores: 'the sisters (the Muses) wept for his
   loss in silent grief'.

30. STATIUS, *THEBAID* 9.885-907: PARTHENOPAEUS' LAST WORDS

The youthful hero Parthenopaeus, mortally wounded, gives his
friend Dorceus a touching last message for his mother Atalanta
whose pleas he had ignored in taking up arms.

885 labimur: 'I am dying' (lit. 'slipping away').

886-887 si vera ... curae: 'if concern brings true prediction'.

888-889 arte pia: 'with loyal deceit'.
trepidam suspende: 'keep her fears in suspense'.

889-891 cogēre: fut. indic. passive.
poenas invita capesse: 'exact punishment, unwilling though you
   be'. *capessere*, 'to seize eagerly, snatch at, lay hold of;
   take in hand, busy onself with, enter upon, engage in; to
   strive to reach, to resort to'; cf. *rem publicam capessere*,
   'to enter public life'.

894-895 animis ... nostris: '(be angry rather) at my impetuous
   spirit'.

898-899 efflantiaque ora: 'my last breath'; *efflare* (mostly in poetry and post-Augustan prose) is used on its own here, though it normally has *animam* (or *halitum extremum*) as object.

900-902 hunc ... crinem: Parthenopaeus bids Dorceus take back a lock of his hair so that his mother may give it a funeral (in place of his body).
hunc toto capies ...: there is humour in this line, as well as pathos - a blend not uncharacteristic of Statius.
frustra: either with *comere* (his hair quickly became disarranged again) or with *dedignante* (protest as he would, his mother would comb his locks).

903-905 iusta: 'funeral ceremonies'.
antris: here 'hunting grounds'; *antrum*, a Greek word introduced into Latin by Virgil (e.g. *Aeneid* 6.11) meaning 'cave, cavern, grotto'; and so anything hollow, 'valley, glen, dell' (cf. Propertius 1.1.11; 4.4.3).

906-907 'but burn these ill-omened arms from my first warfare (*primis ... castris*), or hang them up as an offering to reproach Diana's thankless heart'. Diana was patron goddess of hunters. It was customary, upon retirement, to hang up the tools of one's trade in the temple of that trade's presiding divinity.

31. STATIUS, *THEBAID* 10.137-155: SLEEP FALLS ON THE ARMY

This excerpt is from Book 10 of the *Thebaid* which contains a number of interesting passages: the night fighting and the death of Menoeceus (686-782); the exaggerated and overdrawn exploits of Capaneus (827ff.); and the story of Hopleus and Dymas (347-448), based on Virgil's tale of Nisus and Euryalus (*Aeneid* 9.176ff.) with its ultimate dependence on the story of Dolon (Homer, *Iliad* 10). Perhaps the most appealing and carefully worked passage is that to do with the deity or personification of Sleep.

The attacking forces of Polynices have suffered defeat. The Theban walls are closely guarded by the defending troops of Eteocles. The attackers' fortunes are at a low ebb but they are championed by Juno, who sends her messenger Iris to intervene, as she does in Virgil, *Aeneid* 5.604ff. where she drives the women to burn the Trojan ships. Statius has Iris visit the cave of Sleep which is described in detail (87-117); she rouses him to cause the army inside Thebes to fall asleep and relax their guard (118-136); he does so in this extract which recalls those beautiful lines of Virgil (*Aeneid* 4.522-528 - see Appendix passage r below) of which Heyne (see Austin (1955) n. *ad loc.*) declared: *suavissima noctis descriptio, quae ipsam rerum quietem spirare videtur.* It is night and all the world of nature sleeps - except for Dido; in Statius it is nature and all the army within Thebes that sleeps - except the "Greeks", the besiegers.

This passage and the description of the cave of Sleep which
leads up to it show the extent to which Statius was attracted
by the theme.

Our passage should be compared with *Silvae* 5.4, perhaps Statius'
best-known poem, which appears with full notes in the Appendix
of this volume (passage s below). In form and content it is
rather like a sonnet on sleep and of the imitations and emu-
lations it has inspired most are sonnets; see Appendix to
Oxford Book of Latin Verse where sonnets to sleep by Sidney,
Daniel, Drummond, Wordsworth, Keats and Coleridge are given for
comparison with Statius.

137-140 ipse quoque ...: 'Sleep himself too roused his step to
  flight until the wind swept past his temples and filled his
  bellying cloak with the coolness of the dark sky'. *volucrem:*
  (also *ventosa*) used proleptically.
gravis: lit. 'heavy', here 'making drowsy'.

141-145 Cf. Virgil, *Aeneid* 4.525 - *iam tacet omnis ager, pecudes pic-
  taeque volucres; Silvae* 5.4.3 - Appendix passages r and s below.
explicat: 'laid prostrate'; cf. *Thebaid* 10.277 - *hunc temere
  explicitum stratis* ('this man stretched carelessly on a
  couch').
penitus: with *sidunt* (143) 'subsided completely'.
quemcumque supervolat orbem: 'over whatsoever part of the
  world he passed in flight'.
cacumina: 'tree-tops'; cf. (in same sense) *Silvae* 5.4.4 (Appendix
  passage s below).
pluraque laxato ceciderunt sidera caelo: 'golden' line in the
  form *a b* verb *a b*. Also typically Statian and Silver epic
  exaggeration; the sky, relaxed in repose, cannot hold the
  stars.

146-148 submisere sonum: 'were hushed'.

148-151 incubuit: 'bore down upon them'; *incumbere*: often used
  of the action of winds and storms ('to swoop down upon');
  cf. e.g. Virgil, *Aeneid* 1.84; 12.367; *Georgics* 2.311; 3.197;
  Valerius Flaccus 2.60.
haud umquam densior: 'darker (lit. 'thicker') than ever before
  with his pitchblack shadow'; cf. Lucan 5.166 - *non umquam
  plenior* ('more fully than ever before').
subit: perfect, contracted form for *subiit.*
errare: historic infinitive (also *relinqui* - 151), quite common
  in Statius and Virgil, less so in Ovid.
resolutaque colla: 'heads sank'; cf. Virgil, *Aeneid* 6.422 (of
  Cerberus asleep) - *immania terga resolvit.*

152-153 pila: anachronistic; the *pilum* was the characteristic
  weapon of the Roman army.

155 cornipedes: see passage 28.391 n. above.
abstulit: 'quenched'.

32. STATIUS, *ACHILLEID* 1.363-378:   ACHILLES IN DISGUISE

Thetis introduces her son, the youthful Achilles, disguised as
a girl, to the company of Lycomedes and his daughters in Scyros.
Her object in so doing is to prevent his being conscripted
for service in the war against Troy.   The existing completed
part of the *Achilleid* tells how he was discovered and unmasked.
The extract includes (372-378) a pleasing and extended simile
comparing the dance of the Scyrian maidens, which Achilles has
just joined, to a flock of doves (see 372 n. below) fluttering
to their resting-place.

363-364 pater: Lycomedes; 'the father accedes to her words'.
occultum Aeaciden: 'Achilles (son of Aeacus) in disguise'.

365-369 grates electus agit: lit. 'having been chosen gives
    thanks', i.e. 'gives thanks that he has been chosen' (to
    receive and look after Achilles).
defigere: 'stare at', here with *ora* (368); normal usage is
    oculos defigere.
fundat: 'extends' (from *fundere*).   The indirect question arises
    from the curiosity implied in *defigere ora*.   The disguised
    Achilles makes a strapping lass.

370-371 sociare choros: 'join them in the dancing' (lit. 'join
    his - or, rather, her - dancing to theirs').
ceduntque loco: 'they make way for her'.
contingere gaudent: 'they are glad to be near her'; cf. Virgil,
    Aeneid 2.239 - *funemque manu contingere gaudent* (the happy
    people of Troy helping to drag the Wooden Horse into the city).

372-375 Idaliae volucres: 'Idalian birds' - i.e. doves, sacred
    to Venus who had a shrine at Idalium.
iam longum caeloque domoque gregatae: 'after having for long
    been congregated in their skyey home' (*caeloque domoque*,
    hendiadys).   *gregatae:* the only instance in classical Latin
    of the simple (non-compound) verb *gregare*.
si iunxit pinnas: 'if (a strange bird - *hospita avis*) has joined
    them wing to wing'.

376-378 fecere: customary perfect (or 'aorist').
plausuque secundo: 'and with favourable beating of wings'.

APPENDIX

This Appendix prints some passages to which reference is
made (by letter) in the Introduction and in the Com-
mentary. Its main purpose is to give for comparison
passages of Virgil which the writers of Silver Epic
were reworking. In two instances (e and g) lines from
Ennius' *Annales* are also given. Ennius and Virgil were
in turn frequently indebted to Homer and salient references
are given in the notes. In four cases (c, e, g and s)
parallels from Ovid's *Metamorphoses* and from Silver Latin
poetry are also given for comparison.

a. Virgil, *Georgics* 1.24-42

```
tuque adeo, quem mox quae sint habitura deorum
concilia incertum est, urbisne invisere, Caesar,        25
terrarumque velis curam, et te maximus orbis
auctorem frugum tempestatumque potentem
accipiat cingens materna tempora myrto;
an deus immensi venias maris ac tua nautae
numina sola colant, tibi serviat ultima Thule,          30
teque sibi generum Tethys emat omnibus undis;
anne novum tardis sidus te mensibus addas,
qua locus Erigonen inter Chelasque sequentis
panditur (ipse tibi iam bracchia contrahit ardens
Scorpius et caeli iusta plus parte reliquit);           35
quidquid eris (nam te nec sperant Tartara regem,
nec tibi regnandi veniat tam dira cupido,
quamvis Elysios miretur Graecia campos
nec repetita sequi curet Proserpina matrem),
da facilem cursum atque audacibus adnue coeptis,        40
ignarosque viae mecum miseratus agrestis
ingredere et votis iam nunc adsuesce vocari.
```

b. Virgil, *Aeneid* 11.631-635

```
tertia sed postquam congressi in proelia totas
implicuere inter se acies legitque virum vir,
tum vero et gemitus morientum et sanguine in alto
armaque corporaque et permixti caede virorum
semianimes volvuntur equi, pugna aspera surgit.         635
```

c. Virgil, *Aeneid* 4.173-188

```
extemplo Libyae magnas it Fama per urbes,
Fama, malum qua non aliud velocius ullum:
mobilitate viget virisque adquirit eundo,               175
parva metu primo, mox sese attollit in auras
ingrediturque solo et caput inter nubila condit.
illam Terra parens ira inritata deorum
extremam, ut perhibent, Coeo Enceladoque sororem
progenuit pedibus celerem et pernicibus alis,           180
monstrum horrendum, ingens, cui quot sunt corpore plumae,
tot vigiles oculi subter (mirabile dictu),
tot linguae, totidem ora sonant, tot subrigit auris.
nocte volat caeli medio terraeque per umbram
stridens, nec dulci declinat lumina somno;              185
luce sedet custos aut summi culmine tecti
turribus aut altis, et magnas territat urbes,
tam ficti pravique tenax quam nuntia veri.
```

cf. Ovid, *Metamorphoses* 9.136-140

       victor ab Oechalia Cenaeo sacra parabat
       vota Iovi, cum Fama loquax praecessit ad aures,
       Deianira, tuas, quae veris addere falsa
       gaudet, et e minimo sua per mendacia crescit,
       Amphitryoniaden Ioles ardore teneri.   140

cf. Ovid, *Metamorphoses* 12.39-63

       orbe locus medio est inter terrasque fretumque
       caelestesque plagas, triplicis confinia mundi;   40
       unde quod est usquam, quamvis regionibus absit,
       inspicitur, penetratque cavas vox omnis ad aures:
       Fama tenet summaque domum sibi legit in arce,
       innumerosque aditus ac mille foramina tectis
       addidit et nullis inclusit limina portis;   45
       nocte dieque patet: tota est ex aere sonanti,
       tota fremit vocesque refert iteratque quod audit;
       nulla quies intus nullaque silentia parte,
       nec tamen est clamor, sed parvae murmura vocis,
       qualia de pelagi, siquis procul audiat, undis   50
       esse solent, qualemve sonum, cum Iuppiter atras
       increpuit nubes, extrema tonitrua reddunt.
       atria turba tenet: veniunt, leve vulgus, euntque
       mixtaque cum veris passim commenta vagantur
       milia rumorum confusaque verba volutant;   55
       e quibus hi vacuas inplent sermonibus aures,
       hi narrata ferunt alio, mensuraque ficti
       crescit, et auditis aliquid novus adicit auctor.
       illic Credulitas, illic temerarius Error
       vanaque Laetitia est consternatique Timores   60
       Seditioque recens dubioque auctore Susurri;
       ipsa, quid in caelo rerum pelagoque geratur
       et tellure, videt totumque inquirit in orbem.

cf. Valerius Flaccus, *Argonautica* 2.115-125

       cum dea se piceo per sudum turbida nimbo   115
       praecipitat Famamque vagam vestigat in umbra,
       quam pater omnipotens digna atque indigna canentem
       spargentemque metus placidis regionibus arcet
       aetheris: illa fremens habitat sub nubibus imis,
       non erebi, non diva poli, terrasque fatigat,   120
       quas datur; auditam primi spernuntque foventque;
       mox omnes agit et motis quatit oppida linguis.
       talem diva sibi scelerisque dolique ministram
       quaerit avens. videt illa prior, iamque advolat ultro
       impatiens, iamque ora parat, iam suscitat aures.   125

cf. Silius Italicus, *Punica* 6.552-554

> interea, rapidas perfusa cruoribus alas,
> sicut sanguinea Thrasymenni tinxerat unda,
> vera ac ficta simul spargebat Fama per urbem.

d.   Virgil, *Georgics* 1.463-492

```
                        solem quis dicere falsum
audeat?  ille etiam caecos instare tumultus
saepe monet fraudemque et operta tumescere bella;      465
ille etiam exstincto miseratus Caesare Romam,
cum caput obscura nitidum ferrugine texit
impiaque aeternam timuerunt saecula noctem.
tempore quamquam illo tellus quoque et aequora ponti,
obscenaeque canes importunaeque volucres               470
signa dabant.  quotiens Cyclopum effervere in agros
vidimus undantem ruptis fornacibus Aetnam,
flammarumque globos liquefactaque volvere saxa!
armorum sonitum toto Germania caelo
audiit, insolitis tremuerunt motibus Alpes.            475
vox quoque per lucos vulgo exaudita silentis
ingens, et simulacra modis pallentia miris
visa sub obscurum noctis, pecudesque locutae
(infandum!); sistunt amnes terraeque dehiscunt,
et maestum inlacrimat templis ebur aeraque sudant.     480
proluit insano contorquens vertice silvas
fluviorum rex Eridanus camposque per omnis
cum stabulis armenta tulit.  nec tempore eodem
tristibus aut extis fibrae apparere minaces
aut puteis manare cruor cessavit, et altae             485
per noctem resonare lupis ululantibus urbes.
non alias caelo ceciderunt plura sereno
fulgura nec diri totiens arsere cometae.
ergo inter sese paribus concurrere telis
Romanas acies iterum videre Philippi;                  490
nec fuit indignum superis bis sanguine nostro
Emathiam et latos Haemi pinguescere campos.
```

e.   Virgil, *Aeneid* 6.179-182

```
itur in antiquam silvam, stabula alta ferarum;
procumbunt piceae, sonat icta securibus ilex           180
fraxineaeque trabes cuneis et fissile robur
scinditur, advolvunt ingentis montibus ornos.
```

cf. Virgil, *Aeneid* 11.135-138

```
                ferro sonat alta bipenni                135
fraxinus, evertunt actas ad sidera pinus,
robora nec cuneis et olentem scindere cedrum
nec plaustris cessant vectare gementibus ornos.
```

cf. Ennius, *Annales* (6.) 187-191 (Warmington)

    incedunt arbusta per alta, securibus caedunt.
    percellunt magnas quercus, exciditur ilex,
    fraxinus frangitur atque abies consternitur alta,
    pinus proceras pervortunt; omne sonabat   190
    arbustum fremitu silvai frondosai.

cf. Ovid, *Metamorphoses* 8.741-750 & 774-776

    ille etiam Cereale nemus violasse securi
    dicitur et lucos ferro temerasse vetustos.
    stabat in his ingens annoso robore quercus,
    una nemus; vittae mediam memoresque tabellae
    sertaque cingebant, voti argumenta potentis.   745
    saepe sub hac dryades festas duxere choreas,
    saepe etiam manibus nexis ex ordine trunci
    circuiere modum, mensuraque roboris ulnas
    quinque ter inplebat, nec non et cetera tantum
    silva sub hac, silva quantum fuit herba sub omni.   750

    persequitur scelus ille suum, labefactaque tandem
    ictibus innumeris adductaque funibus arbor   775
    corruit et multam prostravit pondere silvam.

cf. Statius, *Thebaid* 12.50-56

    tertius Aurorae pugnabat Lucifer, et iam   50
    montibus orbatis, lucorum gloria, magnae
    Teumesi venere trabes et amica Cithaeron
    silva rogis; arlent excisae viscera gentis
    molibus exstructis: supremo munere gaudent
    Ogygii manes; queritur miserabile Graium   55
    nuda cohors vetitumque gemens circumvolat ignem.

f. Virgil, *Aeneid* 6.42-103

    excisum Euboicae latus ingens rupis in antrum,
    quo lati ducunt aditus centum, ostia centum,
    unde ruunt totidem voces, responsa Sibyllae.
    ventum erat ad limen, cum virgo 'poscere fata   45
    tempus' ait; 'deus ecce deus!' cui talia fanti
    ante fores subito non vultus, non color unus,
    non comptae mansere comae; sed pectus anhelum,
    et rabie fera corda tument, maiorque videri
    nec mortale sonans, adflata est numine quando   50
    iam propiore dei. 'cessas in vota precesque,
    Tros' ait 'Aenea? cessas? neque enim ante dehiscent
    attonitae magna ora domus.' et talia fata
    conticuit. gelidus Teucris per dura cucurrit

ossa tremor, funditque preces rex pectore ab imo: 55
'Phoebe, gravis Troiae semper miserate labores,
Dardana qui Paridis derexti tela manusque
corpus in Aeacidae, ·magnas obeuntia terras
tot maria intravi duce te penitusque repostas
Massylum gentis praetentaque Syrtibus arva: 60
iam tandem Italiae fugientis prendimus oras.
hac Troiana tenus fuerit fortuna secuta;
vos quoque Pergameae iam fas est parcere genti,
dique deaeque omnes, quibus obstitit Ilium et ingens
gloria Dardaniae. tuque, o sanctissima vates,   65
praescia venturi, da (non indebita posco
regna meis fatis) Latio considere Teucros
errantisque deos agitataque numina Troiae.
tum Phoebo et Triviae solido de marmore templum
instituam festosque dies de nomine Phoebi.   70
te quoque magna manent regnis penetralia nostris:
hic ego namque tuas sortis arcanaque fata
dicta meae genti ponam, lectosque sacrabo,
alma, viros. foliis tantum ne carmina manda,
ne turbata volent rapidis ludibria ventis;   75
ipsa canas oro.' finem dedit ore loquendi.
    at Phoebi nondum patiens immanis in antro
bacchatur vates, magnum si pectore possit
excussisse deum; tanto magis ille fatigat
os rabidum, fera corda domans, fingitque premendo.   80
ostia iamque domus patuere ingentia centum
sponte sua vatisque ferunt responsa per auras:
'o tandem magnis pelagi defuncte periclis
(sed terrae graviora manent), in regna Lavini
Dardanidae venient (mitte hanc de pectore curam),   85
sed non et venisse volent. bella, horrida bella,
et Thybrim multo spumantem sanguine cerno.
non Simois tibi nec Xanthus nec Dorica castra
defuerint; alius Latio iam partus Achilles,
natus et ipse dea; nec Teucris addita Iuno   90
usquam aberit, cum tu supplex in rebus egenis
quas gentis Italum aut quas non oraveris urbes!
causa mali tanti coniunx iterum hospita Teucris
externique iterum thalami.
tu ne cede malis, sed contra audentior ito,   95
qua tua te Fortuna sinet. via prima salutis
(quod minime reris) Graia pandetur ab urbe.'
    talibus ex adyto dictis Cumaea Sibylla
horrendas canit ambages antroque remugit,
obscuris vera involvens: ea frena furenti   100
concutit et stimulos sub pectore vertit Apollo.
ut primum cessit furor et rabida ora quierunt,
incipit Aeneas heros:

g. Virgil, *Aeneid* 1.81-123

　　　haec ubi dicta, cavum conversa cuspide montem
　　　impulit in latus; ac venti velut agmine facto,
　　　qua data porta, ruunt et terras turbine perflant.
　　　incubuere mari totumque a sedibus imis
　　　una Eurusque Notusque ruunt creberque procellis　　　85
　　　Africus, et vastos volvunt ad litora fluctus.
　　　insequitur clamorque virum stridorque rudentum;
　　　eripiunt subito nubes caelumque diemque
　　　Teucrorum ex oculis; ponto nox incubat atra;
　　　intonuere poli et crebris micat ignibus aether　　　90
　　　praesentemque viris intentant omnia mortem.
　　　extemplo Aeneae solvuntur frigore membra;
　　　ingemit et duplicis tendens ad sidera palmas
　　　talia voce refert: 'o terque quaterque beati,
　　　quis ante ora patrum Troiae sub moenibus altis　　　95
　　　contigit oppetere! o Danaum fortissime gentis
　　　Tydide! mene Iliacis occumbere campis
　　　non potuisse tuaque animam hanc effundere dextra,
　　　saevus ubi Aeacidae telo iacet Hector, ubi ingens
　　　Sarpedon, ubi tot Simois correpta sub undis　　　100
　　　scuta virum galeasque et fortia corpora volvit!'
　　　　talia iactanti stridens Aquilone procella
　　　velum adversa ferit, fluctusque ad sidera tollit.
　　　franguntur remi, tum prora avertit et undis
　　　dat latus, insequitur cumulo praeruptus aquae mons.　105
　　　hi summo in fluctu pendent; his unda dehiscens
　　　terram inter fluctus aperit, furit aestus harenis.
　　　tris Notus abreptas in saxa latentia torquet
　　　(saxa vocant Itali mediis quae in fluctibus Aras,
　　　dorsum immane mari summo), tris Eurus ab alto　　　110
　　　in brevia et syrtis urget, miserabile visu,
　　　inliditque vadis atque aggere cingit harenae.
　　　unam, quae Lycios fidumque vehebat Oronten,
　　　ipsius ante oculos ingens a vertice pontus
　　　in puppim ferit: excutitur pronusque magister　　　115
　　　volvitur in caput, ast illam ter fluctus ibidem
　　　torquet agens circum et rapidus vorat aequore vertex.
　　　apparent rari nantes in gurgite vasto,
　　　arma virum tabulaeque et Troia gaza per undas.
　　　iam validam Ilionei navem, iam fortis Achatae,　　　120
　　　et qua vectus Abas, et qua grandaevus Aletes,
　　　vicit hiems; laxis laterum compagibus omnes
　　　accipiunt inimicum imbrem rimisque fatiscunt.

cf. Ennius, *Annales* (17.) 430-432 (Warmington)

　　　concurrunt veluti venti quom spiritus Austri　　　430
　　　imbricitor Aquiloque suo cum flamine contra
　　　indu mari magno fluctus extollere certant.

cf. Ovid, *Metamorphoses* 11.474-543

```
portibus exierant, et moverat aura rudentes:
obvertit lateri pendentes navita remos                          475
cornuaque in summa locat arbore totaque malo
carbasa deducit venientesque accipit auras.
aut minus, aut certe medium non amplius aequor
puppe secabatur, longeque erat utraque tellus,
cum mare sub noctem tumidis albescere coepit              480
fluctibus et praeceps spirare valentius Eurus.
"ardua iamdudum demittite cornua" rector
clamat "et antemnis totum subnectite velum."
hic iubet; inpediunt adversae iussa procellae,
nec sinit audiri vocem fragor aequoris ullam:             485
sponte tamen properant alii subducere remos,
pars munire latus, pars ventis vela negare;
egerit hic fluctus aequorque refundit in aequor,
hic rapit antemnas; quae dum sine lege geruntur,
aspera crescit hiems, omnique e parte feroces            490
bella gerunt venti fretaque indignantia miscent.
ipse pavet nec se, qui sit status, ipse fatetur
scire ratis rector, nec quid iubeatve vetetve:
tanta mali moles tantoque potentior arte est.
quippe sonant clamore viri, stridore rudentes,           495
undarum incursu gravis unda, tonitribus aether.
fluctibus erigitur caelumque aequare videtur
pontus et inductas aspergine tangere nubes;
et modo, cum fulvas ex imo vertit harenas,
concolor est illis, Stygia modo nigrior unda,            500
sternitur interdum spumisque sonantibus albet.
ipsa quoque his agitur vicibus Trachinia puppis
et nunc sublimis veluti de vertice montis
despicere in valles imumque Acheronta videtur,
nunc, ubi demissam curvum circumstetit aequor,           505
suspicere inferno summum de gurgite caelum.
saepe dat ingentem fluctu latus icta fragorem
nec levius pulsata sonat, quam ferreus olim
cum laceras aries balistave concutit arces,
utque solent sumptis incursu viribus ire                 510
pectore in arma feri protentaque tela leones,
sic, ubi se ventis admiserat unda coortis,
ibat in arma ratis multoque erat altior illis;
iamque labant cunei, spoliataque tegmine cerae
rima patet praebetque viam letalibus undis.              515
ecce cadunt largi resolutis nubibus imbres,
inque fretum credas totum descendere caelum,
inque plagas caeli tumefactum ascendere pontum.
vela madent nimbis, et cum caelestibus undis
aequoreae miscentur aquae; caret ignibus aether,         520
caecaque nox premitur tenebris hiemisque suisque.
discutiunt tamen has praebentque micantia lumen
fulmina: fulmineis ardescunt ignibus undae.
dat quoque iam saltus intra cava texta carinae
```

```
fluctus; et ut miles, numero praestantior omni,              525
cum saepe adsiluit defensae moenibus urbis,
spe potitur tandem laudisque accensus amore
inter mille viros murum tamen occupat unus,
sic ubi pulsarunt noviens latera ardua fluctus,
vastius insurgens decimae ruit impetus undae               530
nec prius absistit fessam oppugnare carinam,
quam velut in captae descendat moenia navis.
pars igitur temptabat adhuc invadere pinum,
pars maris intus erat: trepidant haud setius omnes,
quam solet urbs aliis murum fodientibus extra             535
atque aliis murum trepidare tenentibus intus.
deficit ars, animique cadunt, totidemque videntur,
quot veniunt fluctus, ruere atque inrumpere mortes.
non tenet hic lacrimas, stupet hic, vocat ille beatos,
funera quos maneant, hic votis numen adorat              540
bracchiaque ad caelum, quod non videt, inrita tollens
poscit opem; subeunt illi fraterque parensque,
huic cum pignoribus domus et quodcunque relictum est;
```

h.   Virgil, *Georgics* 1.427-433

```
luna revertentis cum primum colligit ignis,
si nigrum obscuro comprenderit aëra cornu,
maximus agricolis pelagoque parabitur imber;
at si virgineum suffuderit ore ruborem,                    430
ventus erit: vento semper rubet aurea Phoebe.
sin ortu quarto (namque is certissimus auctor)
pura neque obtunsis per caelum cornibus ibit.
```

i.   Virgil, *Aeneid* 5.13-25

```
'heu quianam tanti cinxerunt aethera nimbi?
quidve, pater Neptune, paras?' sic deinde locutus
colligere arma iubet validisque incumbere remis,          15
obliquatque sinus in ventum ac talia fatur:
'magnanime Aenea, non, si mihi Iuppiter auctor
spondeat, hoc sperem Italiam contingere caelo.
mutati transversa fremunt et vespere ab atro
consurgunt venti, atque in nubem cogitur aër.             20
nec nos obniti contra nec tendere tantum
sufficimus. superat quoniam Fortuna, sequamur,
quoque vocat vertamus iter. nec litora longe
fida reor fraterna Erycis portusque Sicanos,
si modo rite memor servata remetior astra.'               25
```

j.   Virgil, *Aeneid* 2.554-558

```
haec finis Priami fatorum, hic exitus illum
sorte tulit Troiam incensam et prolapsa videntem          555
```

Pergama, tot quondam populis terrisque superbum
regnatorem Asiae. iacet ingens litore truncus,
avulsumque umeris caput et sine nomine corpus.

k. Virgil, *Aeneid* 6.14-41

Daedalus, ut fama est, fugiens Minoia regna
praepetibus pennis ausus se credere caelo   15
insuetum per iter gelidas enavit ad Arctos,
Chalcidicaque levis tandem super astitit arce.
redditus his primum terris tibi, Phoebe, sacravit
remigium alarum posuitque immania templa.
in foribus letum Androgeo; tum pendere poenas   20
Cecropidae iussi (miserum!) septena quotannis
corpora natorum; stat ductis sortibus urna.
contra elata mari respondet Cnosia tellus:
hic crudelis amor tauri suppostaque furto
Pasiphae mixtumque genus prolesque biformis   25
Minotaurus inest, Veneris monimenta nefandae,
hic labor ille domus et inextricabilis error;
magnum reginae sed enim miseratus amorem
Daedalus ipse dolos tecti ambagesque resolvit,
caeca regens filo vestigia. tu quoque magnam   30
partem opere in tanto, sineret dolor, Icare, haberes.
bis conatus erat casus effingere in auro,
bis patriae cecidere manus. quin protinus omnia
perlegerent oculis, ni iam praemissus Achates
adforet atque una Phoebi Triviaeque sacerdos,   35
Deiphobe Glauci, fatur quae talia regi:
'non hoc ista sibi tempus spectacula poscit;
nunc grege de intacto septem mactare iuvencos
praestiterit, totidem lectas ex more bidentis.'
talibus adfata Aenean (nec sacra morantur   40
iussa viri) Teucros vocat alta in templa sacerdos.

l. Virgil, *Aeneid* 4.300-303

saevit inops animi totamque incensa per urbem   300
bacchatur, qualis commotis excita sacris
Thyias, ubi audito stimulant trieterica Baccho
orgia nocturnusque vocat clamore Cithaeron.

m. Virgil, *Aeneid* 4.1-30

at regina gravi iamdudum saucia cura
vulnus alit venis et caeco carpitur igni.
multa viri virtus animo multusque recursat
gentis honos; haerent infixi pectore vultus
verbaque nec placidam membris dat cura quietem.   5
postera Phoebea lustrabat lampade terras
umentemque Aurora polo dimoverat umbram,

cum sic unanimam adloquitur male sana sororem:
'Anna soror, quae me suspensam insomnia terrent!
quis novus hic nostris successit sedibus hospes,   10
quem sese ore ferens, quam forti pectore et armis!
credo equidem, nec vana fides, genus esse deorum.
degeneres animos timor arguit. heu, quibus ille
iactatus fatis! quae bella exhausta canebat!
si mihi non animo fixum immotumque sederet   15
ne cui me vincio vellem sociare iugali,
postquam primus amor deceptam morte fefellit;
si non pertaesum thalami taedaeque fuisset,
huic uni forsan potui succumbere culpae.
Anna (fatebor enim) miseri post fata Sychaei   20
coniugis et sparsos fraterna caede penatis
solus hic inflexit sensus animumque labantem
impulit. agnosco veteris vestigia flammae.
sed mihi vel tellus optem prius ima dehiscat
vel pater omnipotens adigat me fulmine ad umbras,   25
pallentis umbras Erebo noctemque profundam,
ante, pudor, quam te violo aut tua iura resolvo.
ille meos, primus qui me sibi iunxit, amores
abstulit; ille habeat secum servetque sepulcro.'
sic effata sinum lacrimis implevit obortis.   30

n.   Virgil, *Aeneid* 6.445-474

his Phaedram Procrimque locis maestamque Eriphylen   445
crudelis nati monstrantem vulnera cernit,
Evadnenque et Pasiphaen; his Laodamia
it comes et iuvenis quondam, nunc femina, Caeneus
rursus et in veterem fato revoluta figuram.
inter quas Phoenissa recens a vulnere Dido   450
errabat silva in magna; quam Troius heros
ut primum iuxta stetit agnovitque per umbras
obscuram, qualem primo qui surgere mense
aut videt aut vidisse putat per nubila lunam,
demisit lacrimas dulcique adfatus amore est: 455
'infelix Dido, verus mihi nuntius ergo
venerat exstinctam ferroque extrema secutam?
funeris heu tibi causa fui? per sidera iuro,
per superos et si qua fides tellure sub ima est,
invitus, regina, tuo de litore cessi.   460
sed me iussa deum, quae nunc has ire per umbras,
per loca senta situ cogunt noctemque profundam,
imperiis egere suis; nec credere quivi
hunc tantum tibi me discessu ferre dolorem.
siste gradum teque aspectu ne subtrahe nostro.   465
quem fugis? extremum fato quod te adloquor hoc est.'
talibus Aeneas ardentem et torva tuentem
lenibat dictis animum lacrimasque ciebat.
illa solo fixos oculos aversa tenebat
nec magis incepto vultum sermone movetur   470

quam si dura silex aut stet Marpesia cautes.
tandem corripuit sese atque inimica refugit
in nemus umbriferum, coniunx ubi pristinus illi
respondet curis aequatque Sychaeus amorem.

p.   Virgil, *Aeneid* 11.522-531

est curvo anfractu valles, accommoda fraudi
armorumque dolis, quam densis frondibus atrum
urget utrimque latus, tenuis quo semita ducit
angustaeque ferunt fauces aditusque maligni.   525
hanc super in speculis summoque in vertice montis
planities ignota iacet tutique receptus,
seu dextra laevaque velis occurrere pugnae
sive instare iugis et grandia volvere saxa.
huc iuvenis nota fertur regione viarum   530
arripuitque locum et silvis insedit iniquis.

q.   Virgil, *Aeneid* 6.212-235

nec minus interea Misenum in litore Teucri
flebant et cineri ingrato suprema ferebant.
principio pinguem taedis et robore secto
ingentem struxere pyram, cui frondibus atris   215
intexunt latera et feralis ante cupressos
constituunt, decorantque super fulgentibus armis.
pars calidos latices et aëna undantia flammis
expediunt, corpusque lavant frigentis et unguunt.
fit gemitus. tum membra toro defleta reponunt   220
purpureasque super vestis, velamina nota,
coniciunt. pars ingenti subiere feretro,
triste ministerium, et subiectam more parentum
aversi tenuere facem. congesta cremantur
turea dona, dapes, fuso crateres olivo.   225
postquam conlapsi cineres et flamma quievit,
reliquias vino et bibulam lavere favillam,
ossaque lecta cado texit Corynaeus aëno.
idem ter socios pura circumtulit unda
spargens rore levi et ramo felicis olivae,   230
lustravitque viros dixitque novissima verba.
at pius Aeneas ingenti mole sepulcrum
imponit suaque arma viro remumque tubamque
monte sub aërio, qui nunc Misenus ab illo
dicitur aeternumque tenet per saecula nomen.   235

r.   Virgil, *Aeneid* 4.522-527

nox erat et placidum carpebant fessa soporem
corpora per terras, silvaeque et saeva quierant
aequora, cum medio volvuntur sidera lapsu,
cum tacet omnis ager, pecudes pictaeque volucres,   525

quaeque lacus late liquidos quaeque aspera dumis
rura tenent, somno positae sub nocte silenti.

s.   Statius, *Silvae* 5.4 (to Sleep)

crimine quo merui, iuvenis placidissime divum,
quove errore miser, donis ut solus egerem,
Somne, tuis? tacet omne pecus volucresque feraeque
et simulant fessos curvata cacumina somnos,
nec trucibus fluviis idem sonus; occidit horror   5
aequoris, et terris maria adclinata quiescunt.
septima iam rediens Phoebe mihi respicit aegras
stare genas; totidem Oetaeae Paphiaeque revisunt
lampades et totiens nostros Tithonia questus
praeterit et gelido spargit miserata flagello.   10
unde ego sufficiam? non si mihi lumina mille,
quae sacer alterna tantum statione tenebat
Argus et haud umquam vigilabat corpore toto.
at nunc heu! si aliquis longa sub nocte puellae
brachia nexa tenens ultro te, Somne, repellit,   15
inde veni nec te totas infundere pennas
luminibus compello meis - hoc turba precetur
laetior -: extremo me tange cacumine virgae,
sufficit, aut leviter suspenso poplite transi.

4-6   cacumina: 'tree tops', not 'mountains' - cf. passage
       31 above, line 144.
       occidit horror / aequoris: 'the ruffled surface of the
       sea has sunk to rest' - *horrere* = 'to bristle, to be
       rough'.

7-10   respicit aegras / stare genas: 'she beholds my fixed and
       weary eyes' - *gena* 'cheek; socket of the eye, eye'.
       Oetaeae Paphiaeque ... lampades: the evening and the
       morning star. Mount Oeta was conventionally associated
       with the rising of the evening star - cf. Virgil,
       Eclogues 8.30. Paphos was a city in Cyprus and an
       important centre for the worship of Venus, and *Paphiae
       lampades* refers to the planet Venus which, according to
       its position, can be the evening or (as here) the morn-
       ing star.
       Tithonia: i.e. Aurora (the dawn).
       gelido ... flagello: Aurora as a charioteer gives Statius
       the usual charioteer's salute (cf. Juvenal 8.153) with
       her whip, thus flicking on to him some of her dew.

10-13 unde ego sufficiam?: 'where shall I find the strength to
       endure?'. He cannot enjoy a partial sleep like Argus
       who kept each of his hundred (Statius' *mille* is an
       exaggeration, but can simply mean 'countless' as well
       as 'thousand') eyes on guard only half the time.

14-19 luminibus compello meis: for a clear and brief history
of the shortening of final -ŏ of verbs and nouns in
Latin verse see Austin (1964) on Virgil, *Aeneid* 2.735.
extremo ... cacumine virgae: 'with the extremest tip
of your wand'.
aut leviter suspenso poplite transi: *poples, -itis,* m.,
'hollow of the knee, knee' - tr. 'pass over me with
lightly hovering (*suspenso*) step'.